AMERICAN DEMOCRACY: STATE AND LOCAL GOVERNMENT

American Democracy: State and Local Government

Second Edition

HENRY A. TURNER

University of California,
Santa Barbara

Harper & Row, Publishers
New York, Evanston, and London

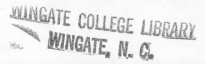

CONTENTS

PREFACE

In this second edition, as in the first, an effort has been made to provide a comprehensive and yet concise treatment of all major aspects of state and local government. This book has been written primarily for college introductory courses in American government. In planning the book the author has assumed that in most instances it will be used in conjunction with a national government text—such as *American Democracy in World Perspective, Second Edition,* by William Ebenstein, C. Herman Pritchett, Henry A. Turner, and Dean Mann—and that many instructors will want to supplement the material with lectures or assigned readings on their own state and local governments. Consequently, topics customarily covered in national government books have been excluded and relatively little information has been presented regarding any particular state. Although only two years have elapsed since the publication of the first edition, all chapters have been up-dated and new material has been added, including a section on state and community politics and party systems. Throughout the book emphasis is placed on the extent to which politics pervades all phases of the governments of states and communities and the importance of these governments in the lives of the American people.

HENRY A. TURNER

AMERICAN DEMOCRACY: STATE AND LOCAL GOVERNMENT

chapter 1

STATE
CONSTITUTIONAL
AND POLITICAL SYSTEMS

The central focus of this book is on the dynamic nature of state and local government and on the importance of government at the "grass roots." In addition to describing and analyzing the political institutions and processes of the states and their local governing units, attention is directed to the more perplexing problems and political issues confronting the state and local communities.

In the past, state and local governments were considered important primarily because they provided such services as education, highways, and police and fire protection. In recent decades government has assumed responsibility in other areas; as a consequence, state and local governments have come to play a greater role in resolving conflicts between various social and economic interests in society. Critical problems facing America today include civil liberties, racial equality, adequate medical care, urban renewal, air and water pollution, and mass rapid-transit systems. Solving these problems requires expenditures of vast sums of money and in some instances the application of technological knowledge and skill by all levels of government. But basically, these are political problems and their solution involves the management of conflicts of interest. Attention is called to the impact of constitutional, organizational, and administrative arrangements on the solution of such pressing public issues. In short, it should be remembered that politics pervades virtually every aspect of state and local government.

The most obvious and significant feature of the American governmental system is the principle of federalism upon which it is based. The Constitution in 1789 established a nation of states—the *United States* of America. Like the governments of Canada, West Germany, and India, American government is based on a division of political authority between the central government and the regional or state governments. This division of authority is provided for in the Constitution of the country and may be changed only by methods specified in that fundamental law. By contrast, in countries with unitary systems of government, such as Great Britain and France, political authority is vested by the fundamental law in the central government, from which local governments derive their powers and even their existence.

Because the thirteen original states existed as colonies prior to the creation of the national government, it would have been unrealistic to propose at the Constitutional Convention, or at any time since, that states be abolished and a unitary form of government be established. If the states had not existed, they undoubtedly would have had to be created, for in a country as large and diverse as the United States, federalism offers many apparent advantages over a unitary government.

For instance, federalism permits the central government to exercise authority over questions of national concern while reserving for the states authority over local matters; it makes possible the decentralization of certain administrative activities and thus helps prevent overburdening the national administrative system; it enables the states and localities to adopt political institutions and procedures that meet their particular needs; it encourages individuals to participate in politics and government at the "grass roots"; and it enables individuals who are politically ambitious to gain experience in state and local positions prior to seeking higher national offices. Moreover, the checks and balances inherent in federalism protect individual rights and help ensure that officials of the central government will act responsibly.

THE FIFTY STATES

The fifty states are characterized by their diversity and variations. Under the federal Constitution each has equal status, but from most other standpoints the states vary greatly. Some of the differences are due to regional influences. Historical events, population characteristics, geography, and economic factors have all contributed to the creation of regional subcultures within the United States. The habits, customs, attitudes, speech patterns, and politics vary considerably among New

England, the Middle West, the South, the Rocky Mountain states and the Pacific states.

States within a given region generally resemble each other more than they do other states; yet, within regions there are dissimilarities, as one may learn by even a superficial comparison of almost any two contiguous states. Compare, for instance, Vermont and Massachusetts, Ohio and Michigan, Florida and Georgia, or Utah and Nevada. Utah, for example, under the influence of the Mormon Church has developed moral and legal codes far different from those of Nevada, which prides itself on being the divorce and gambling center of the nation.

Much has been written regarding the increasing degree of uniformity and conformity within the United States. In recent years, due largely to the migration of people from state to state and the influence of television, attitudes and customs of the American people are becoming more similar across the nation. Yet each of the states is unique; each has developed a distinct political personality.

A glance at a topographical map reveals the tremendous variations in the size and geography of the states. Texas is less than half as large as Alaska, but it is 250 times the size of Rhode Island. Some states have extensive seacoasts, lakes, rivers, or mountains. Others have rolling hills, fertile farm lands, semiarid prairies, or deserts. Natural resources and geographic features have contributed to the varied economies of the states. Several states derive most of their income from agriculture, some are largely industrial, and others have economies based on a combination of industry, commerce, and agriculture. Where one lives in the United States may have a decided impact on his education and level of income. Inhabitants of Connecticut and Delaware have per capita annual incomes approximately twice that of people living in Mississippi and Arkansas. Obviously, the level of income and the state's resources have a direct bearing on how much a state can spend on education, welfare programs, recreational facilities, highways, and other state facilities and activities.

Demographic differences are fully as pronounced as the geographic and economic variations. New York and California have more population each than all but 28 of the more than 125 independent countries of the world. The total population of these two states comprises nearly one-fifth of the nation's inhabitants and is greater than the combined population of the twenty least populous states. (See Figure 1–1.) Whereas the population of some states—including Vermont, West Virginia, and Iowa—has changed very little in recent decades, Florida, Arizona, Nevada, and California have increased their respective populations by approximately 50 percent over a ten-year period. From the standpoint of population

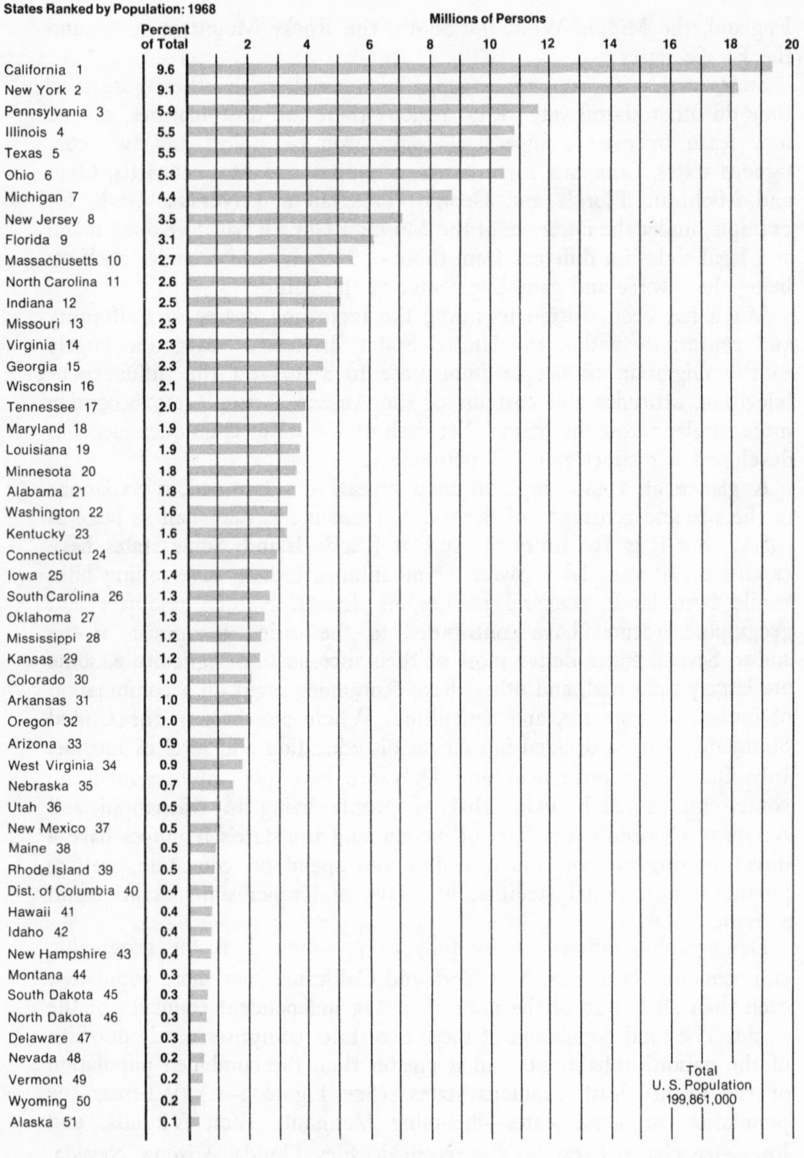

States Ranked by Population: 1968

Millions of Persons

States Ranked by Population	Percent of Total
California 1	9.6
New York 2	9.1
Pennsylvania 3	5.9
Illinois 4	5.5
Texas 5	5.5
Ohio 6	5.3
Michigan 7	4.4
New Jersey 8	3.5
Florida 9	3.1
Massachusetts 10	2.7
North Carolina 11	2.6
Indiana 12	2.5
Missouri 13	2.3
Virginia 14	2.3
Georgia 15	2.3
Wisconsin 16	2.1
Tennessee 17	2.0
Maryland 18	1.9
Louisiana 19	1.9
Minnesota 20	1.8
Alabama 21	1.8
Washington 22	1.6
Kentucky 23	1.6
Connecticut 24	1.5
Iowa 25	1.4
South Carolina 26	1.3
Oklahoma 27	1.3
Mississippi 28	1.2
Kansas 29	1.2
Colorado 30	1.0
Arkansas 31	1.0
Oregon 32	1.0
Arizona 33	0.9
West Virginia 34	0.9
Nebraska 35	0.7
Utah 36	0.5
New Mexico 37	0.5
Maine 38	0.5
Rhode Island 39	0.5
Dist. of Columbia 40	0.4
Hawaii 41	0.4
Idaho 42	0.4
New Hampshire 43	0.4
Montana 44	0.3
South Dakota 45	0.3
North Dakota 46	0.3
Delaware 47	0.3
Nevada 48	0.2
Vermont 49	0.2
Wyoming 50	0.2
Alaska 51	0.1

Total U. S. Population 199,861,000

FIGURE 1–1. States Ranked by Population, July 1, 1968. (*Source:* U.S. Department of Commerce, Bureau of the Census.)

density, the states range from New Jersey with 860 people per square mile to Wyoming and Alaska, which have populations of 3.5 and 0.5 per square mile of territory, respectively. The least urbanized state, North Dakota, has only 35 percent of its people living in urban areas of 2,500 or more population, but in New Jersey nearly nine out of ten individuals live in urban communities.

Persons from virtually every ethnic or racial grouping live in the United States, but they have not spread uniformly throughout the fifty states. There are more Mexican-Americans in the Southwest and more Negroes in the South than elsewhere. In other states large proportions of the population have particular ethnic or nationality backgrounds. In Wisconsin there are many Scandinavians and Germans; New York has large numbers of Irish, Jews, and Italians; Massachusetts has many Irish and Italians; and Hawaii quite naturally is populated by more Orientals than are the other states. Many of the cultural and economic achievements and much of the vitality and progress of the United States may be attributed to the diverse origins of its people.

STATE CONSTITUTIONS

Theoretically, a constitution is a body of basic law. It provides the organizational structure of the government and protects the people against the arbitrary use of governmental power. A constitution should consist of the fundamental principles upon which the government is based, principles which represent the cumulative wisdom of previous generations and are not subject to frequent change. Matters of a transitory nature and governmental details should not be included in a constitution, but should be left to the discretion of the executive and legislative officials. Our national Constitution is an excellent illustration of what a constitution should be. Unfortunately most state constitutions are not.

In the American federal system each state government must function within the fundamental law established by both the national Constitution and its own constitution. The former, in addition to establishing the national government, divides governmental authority between the national and state governments and places certain limitations and obligations on each level of government. Although the United States Constitution delegates certain powers to the national government, it does not specify what functions a state may perform. Instead the states have the reserved or residual powers. The Tenth Amendment states that those "powers not delegated to the United States by the Constitution, nor prohibited by it to the States, are reserved to the States respectively, or to the people." Hence a state, subject to the restrictions imposed by the national Constitution, may draft the kind of constitution it desires.

No other country has had as much experience at drafting constitutions as the United States. In addition to the United States Constitution, every state has drafted at least one constitution, many have adopted as many as six, Georgia is now operating under its eighth, and Louisiana now has its tenth constitution. Together the states have drafted and adopted more than 130 constitutions.

Contents of State Constitutions

Although state constitutions vary greatly in length, they are all similar in basic content. The similarity is due partly to the tendency of constitution framers to borrow from earlier constitutions. The colonial charters served as guides for the first state constitutions written during the Revolutionary War, which in turn have been used as patterns for later constitutions. For example, in 1777 Vermont based its constitution largely on one previously adopted by Pennsylvania; Illinois' first basic law was drawn mainly from Kentucky's and New York's; and more than half of California's first constitution was taken from those of Iowa and New York.

A typical state constitution contains all or most of the following parts or provisions.

Preamble. Constitutions customarily are prefaced with a preamble which sets forth in general terms the purpose of the document. Typically, a preamble will start: "We the people of . . . do ordain and establish. . . ."

Bill of Rights. Every state constitution has a bill of rights, or a declaration of rights, which, like the preamble, is similar to its counterpart in the United States Constitution. Often a state's bill of rights includes more detailed provisions and qualifications than are contained in the federal document. Generally, a state bill of rights protects the traditional rights such as freedom of speech, press, assembly, religion; guarantees the right to a speedy and public trial, due process of law, the right to counsel; and prohibits double jeopardy, self-incrimination, bills of attainder, unreasonable searches and seizures, and the taking of private property for public use without just compensation. Actually many such provisions are unnecessary, for the national Constitution as now interpreted by the courts also protects such rights.

Organization and Functions of Government. The basic document of each state, its constitution, provides for the distribution of governmental functions according to the separation-of-powers doctrine and prescribes the structure, organization, and scope of authority of each of the three branches. Typically, separate sections are devoted to the legislature, the governor and other elective executive officials, and the courts. These sections are often more detailed than the parallel sections of the national Constitution, which specifies only the basic structure and powers of the three branches of government. State constitutions not uncommonly prescribe in detail how the executive branch is to be organized, what powers executive and legislative officials may exercise, and even enumerate specific limitations of the lawmaking authority of the legislature.

In addition to limiting the powers of officials, state constitutions customarily specify what functions the state and local governments are to perform. Many state constitutions contain sections providing for the establishment of certain activities such as public education and public welfare and the regulation or licensing of certain professions, occupations, and industries. State constitutions also customarily contain one section that establishes voting qualifications and the responsibility of certain officials for conducting elections.

Local Government. Most state constitutions provide for the organization and powers of cities, counties, and other units of local government. In some states "home rule" is granted to some cities or counties, but even in those states the constitutions contain provisions applying to other local governments.

The Amending Clause. Constitutions generally specify methods by which they may be amended and the procedure to follow in calling a constitutional convention to draft a new constitution.

Amending State Constitutions

Two steps are required to amend a state constitution. First, an amendment must be proposed; second, it must be ratified.

Proposing Amendments. In all states except New Hampshire constitutional amendments may be proposed by the state legislature.[1] In approximately two-thirds of the states only a single legislature must approve the amendment, but in the remaining states an amendment must be acted upon by two successive legislatures. The vote required in each house to approve constitutional amendments ranges from a simple majority to a three-fifths majority.

---

[1] New Hampshire requires that constitutional amendments originate in a convention.

Thirteen states provide for constitutional amendments to be proposed by the popular initiative. This plan permits a specified number of voters to propose a constitutional amendment by petition and have it submitted to the electorate for approval or rejection. In order for a constitutional amendment to secure a place on the ballot through the initiative, the petition must be signed by qualified voters equal in number to a designated percentage—varying from 8 to 15 percent—of the votes cast in the preceding general election for a specified state official, usually the governor.

Ratification of Amendments. In all states except Delaware constitutional amendments must be ratified by the electorate. In Delaware, amendments adopted by two successive legislatures become part of the constitution without submission to the voters. In most instances the vote required to ratify amendments is only a majority of the votes cast on that amendment. However, in a few states, including Minnesota and Oklahoma, an amendment to be ratified must receive a majority of the votes cast in the election. Since many people vote for candidates but fail to vote on constitutional amendments or other ballot proposals, such a requirement makes it difficult to secure approval for constitutional amendments.

Frequency of Amendment

The states vary greatly from the standpoint of the frequency with which they amend their constitutions. For instance, California has amended its constitution more than 350 times in approximately eighty years, whereas Illinois adopted only 7 amendments in the same number of years. Why, then, are some constitutions amended much more often than others? Obviously, one factor is the ease or difficulty of amendment. Constitutions easily amended are changed more frequently than are others.

The strength and influence of political interest groups in a state also apparently have a bearing on the number of constitutional amendments proposed and adopted.[2] An analysis of a constitution may reveal the more powerful interests in a state—those strong enough to obtain a favored or protected status in the constitution. Where the constitutional initiative is available, as in California, if the legislature refuses to propose an amendment, political interest groups commonly avail themselves of the initiative to secure the amendment they seek. On the other hand, how-

---

[2] Lewis A. Froman, Jr., "Some Effects of Interest Group Strength in State Politics," *American Political Science Review,* LX, No. 4 (December, 1966), 952–962.

ever, if political interest groups are strong in a state, they may experience little difficulty in getting the legislature to propose amendments.

A comparison of state constitutions frequently amended with others that are not reveals that there is a close relationship between the length of a constitution and the number of amendments. The longest state constitution, Louisiana's, has also been amended more frequently than any other, more than 400 times in less than fifty years.

Disadvantages of a Long Constitution

Due both to the length of the original document and to the frequency of amendment, a number of states have extremely long constitutions. Alabama's constitution has more than 80,000 words, and Louisiana's—the longest in the nation—with more than 200,000 words, is twenty-five times the length of the national Constitution.

Long constitutions tend to multiply the problems of all three branches of government. First, lengthy constitutions commonly place limitations on the legislature, the policy-determining branch, which restrict its discretion to enact a balanced and comprehensive program for the state. For instance, as much as a fourth of the annual expenditures in some states are determined by constitutional provisions, thus restricting the power of the legislature to balance and adjust the state's financial policies. One government commission reported: "Perhaps the chief obstacles to legislative flexibility are those created by over-detailed provisions of State Constitutions. . . ." Second, executive officials often are handicapped by provisions of bulky constitutions which place undesirable limitations on their powers and freedom of action. For instance, the governor customarily is responsible for coordinating the work of the state's administrative agencies, but because of insufficient authority and the manner in which the agencies are organized he is seldom able to carry out fully this responsibility. Third, long constitutions place an added burden on the courts; the numerous and detailed provisions of such constitutions present many opportunities for conflicts between the constitution and legislative measures. As Duane Lockard has noted: "Surely the abundance of [constitutional] detail is an open invitation to litigation, and to nullification of legislation.[3] Fourth, the excessive detail and length of such documents make it difficult to determine exactly what the basic law provides on some important subjects. For example, the index to one state constitution lists more than 150 entries under the headings "Taxes" and "Taxation."

[3] Duane Lockard, *The Politics of State and Local Government*, New York: Macmillan, 1969, p. 88.

Constitutional Conventions

If a new constitution or a thorough revision of the existing one is desired, the customary procedure is to call a constitutional convention. In approximately three-fourths of the states the constitutions expressly provide for convening such bodies, and in the other states the power to call a convention has been established by practice or judicial interpretation of the state's basic law.

The commonly accepted procedure for calling a constitutional convention is as follows: First, the legislature proposes to the electorate that a convention be convened. Several state constitutions provide that the question of calling a convention must be submitted to the voters at regular intervals. For example, the question is submitted to the voters every twenty years in Maryland, New York, and several other states; every sixteen years in Michigan; every ten years in Iowa and Alaska; and every seven years in New Hampshire. Second, either a majority voting on the proposal or a majority of those voting in the election must approve calling the convention. Third, the legislature must then provide for the convention and the election of delegates. The number of delegates varies from state to state. Arkansas convention of 1969 was composed of 100 delegates, and the New York convention in 1967 consisted of 186 delegates. The delegates draft the new constitution and submit it to the voters.

In most instances new constitutions may be submitted to the voters as a whole or by separate sections. The argument against the first alternative is that the combined opposition of groups opposed to specific sections may be sufficient to defeat a constitution that would be adopted if submitted section by section. The rejections of new constitutions by the New York voters in 1967 and the Maryland voters in 1968 are illustrative. On the other hand, if submitted by sections, there is the risk that the adoption of some and the rejection of other sections will result in an unbalanced and poorly coordinated document. Submission of the constitution as a whole has been the pattern followed most commonly. Missouri, Georgia, New Jersey, and Michigan, within recent years, have all secured the approval of new constitutions submitted to the voters as single propositions.

Revision by Commission

For more than a century commissions have been used to revise state constitutions. Within the past few years constitutional commissions of one kind or another have been employed in a number of states, including Florida, Kentucky, Pennsylvania, Texas, Wisconsin, and California. The usual procedure for revising a constitution by commission is for the legislature to create a special commission to prepare and present to the legislature a revision of all or part of the state's fundamental law. The legislature may then submit to the voters an amendment or amendments incorporating the commission's recommendations with whatever changes the legislature wishes to make. Thus the legislature retains the right to determine specifically what proposed changes will be presented to the electorate for its approval.

The value of constitutional revision by commission is illustrated by the recent example in California. In 1963 the California legislature established a commission composed of fifty lay members and twenty legislators to prepare and submit to the legislature recommendations for a general revision of the state's basic document. The commission created several subcommittees to study the various parts of the constitution, and a number of consultants were employed. In 1966 the commission issued its first report to the legislature, recommending revisions of sections which together comprised about one-third of the constitution. The legislature, after discussing the recommendations, deferred action on one part of the report but submitted a constitutional amendment incorporating, virtually unchanged, the remaining recommendations. The voters approved the amendment in the general election that year. According to present plans the commission by 1970 will submit reports recommending a revision of the remaining two-thirds of the constitution. If adopted by the legislature and the electorate, these proposals, along with the ones approved in 1966, would provide California an entirely new constitution.

Need for Constitutional Revision

A number of state constitutions today are outmoded and hamper the effective functioning of their state and local governments. In the words of John Buechner, "Most state constitutions today are old, contradictory, lengthy, poorly written, and often inadequate for modern state government."[4] Only about a dozen new state constitutions have been adopted since 1900; Massachusetts' dates back to 1780 and Vermont's to 1793; all of the other state constitutions were adopted during the nineteenth century. One should not assume that because a constitution has been in effect for a long time it should be replaced or thoroughly revised. Our national Constitution illustrates clearly that if a constitution is properly

[4] John C. Buechner, *State Government in the Twentieth Century*, Boston: Houghton Mifflin, 1967, p. 54.

drafted it may admirably serve the needs of the people and be kept up to date by a few amendments.

Unfortunately only a few of the state constitutions meet the needs of their states as well as the federal Constitution serves the nation. Why, then, have more states not adopted new constitutions? The experiences of states indicate that the drafting and adoption of a new constitution is difficult and may be achieved only after several political and psychological barriers are surmounted. In some instances groups with vested interests in the existing constitution have opposed change. The chief psychological obstacle is the apathy and conservatism of the people. Unlike in France where there have been two new constitutions since World War II, in the United States there is a tendency to consider constitutions as sacrosanct. The voters may approve constitutional amendments, but they have evinced little interest in wholesale revision.

An obvious barrier to constitutional revision has been the reluctance of the state legislatures to take the necessary steps to call constitutional conventions or to establish revision commissions, unless required by the constitution to do so. However, within the past few years more than one-third of the states, stimulated in part by the Supreme Court ruling that the state legislatures must be apportioned according to population, have established revision commissions or have called constitution conventions. The fact that a number of states have adopted new and improved constitutions should encourage other states to make the effort. States with outmoded constitutions should heed Thomas Jefferson, who once stated that he was "not an advocate for frequent change in law and constitutions, but . . . with the change of circumstances, institutions must advance also to keep pace with the times."

STATE AND COMMUNITY POLITICS

The federal form of government is responsible for one of the most important features of American political parties, namely, the decentralization of power. In American parties the locus of power is at the state and local levels and not in the national party organization, as in Britain and other countries with unitary governments. Political parties typically organize around the important elective offices, and in the United States all elected officials, except the President and the Vice President, have state or local constituencies. The two major parties, the Republicans and the Democrats, are commonly described as confederations or alliances of state and local party organizations. The "alliance" character of the national parties is illustrated by each state party having the same representation on its national committee regardless of the size of the state, and by the lack of authority of the national party chairman over the state units. Because power in the two major parties is so decentralized, some political observers have asserted that the United States does not have a two-party system, but instead *fifty party systems*.

Despite the decentralization of American political parties, from the standpoint of electoral victories there is a direct relationship between the national party and state party organizations. A highly admired President, for instance, Franklin Roosevelt or Dwight Eisenhower, may add to the support of his party's candidates for state and local offices. Conversely, a presidential nominee with an unpopular program, such as Barry Goldwater in 1964, contributes to the defeat of his party's candidates across the nation. See Table 1–1. But election influence is not entirely unidirectional; strong candidates for such offices as the U.S. Senate or the governorship may help their national ticket carry their state. In some states the election of the principal officials coincides with the presidential election, whereas in other states, these officials are chosen in the off-year elections. Because of the impact of the presidential contest, the party dominant nationally tends to benefit in the states and localities where officials are chosen at the same time as the President.

Fifty Party Systems

American political parties, like those in other countries, have been significantly affected by a variety of historical, demographic, social, and economic factors. For instance, in some states the parties still bear the imprint of the Civil War or the Progressive reform movement, whereas in other states the parties have been affected by the rapid growth of cities, industrial or technological developments, or the ethnic and religious composition of the population.

TABLE 1–1. *Relationship of Gubernatorial to Presidential Elections*

	Presidential and Off-Year Elections	Number of Governors Elected	
		Democrat	Republican
(Eisenhower v. Stevenson)	1956	17	14
	1958	30	9
(Kennedy v. Nixon)	1960	16	12
	1962	25	14
(Johnson v. Goldwater)	1964	18	8
	1966	13	24
(Nixon v. Humphrey)	1968	9	16

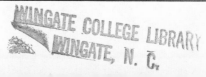

The parties have also been influenced by constitutional and legislative provisions relating to their organizations and activities, for virtually all partisan affairs are regulated by the states. The state defines how an organization becomes legally acknowledged as a party, and how it secures the names of its candidates on the official ballot. In most states for a party to gain legal recognition it must obtain a given percentage of the vote in the preceding gubernatorial election or a certain number of names on a petition. The states and not the parties determine how nominations are made, usually through the open or closed direct primary, although party caucuses or conventions are used in some places. States have attempted to regulate party finance, but with relatively little success. State law also prescribes the method of selecting and the duties of party officials, committees, and conventions. Laws concerning the parties vary considerably from state to state and affect the operation of the parties, as well as account in part for the differences in state party systems.

Although the statutory organizations of the parties in the several states differ, they have common characteristics. Structurally the organizations are based on election districts and follow a pyramidal or hierarchical pattern. Typically, the state legislatures have provided for each official party organization to be headed by a state chairman, a state central committee, and a state convention, with a central committee in each county, and often city, ward, and precinct organizations. These official party organizations are largely responsible for the impression many Americans have that the parties are political "machines" directed from the top, usually by a "boss." During the latter part of the nineteenth century and the early decades of this century bosses controlled parties in a number of cities and in some states, but during recent decades party bosses have been rare.

In actuality, party organizations in most states are weak, exercise little influence, and engage in relatively few political activities. In some states there is little competition for even the top offices in the party organization, and some positions in the organization may go unfilled because of lack of interest in them. Except in the larger states, the party organizations are generally active only during the nomination and election periods. Even during political campaigns the activities of state party organizations differ considerably from one state to another with the general trend toward a reduced role for the official party organization. Many candidates rely very little on the party organizations, but instead create personal campaign organizations composed largely of friends and supporters. Campaign managers and chairmen may be selected primarily because of their status in the community rather than their standing in the party, and in several of the larger states the actual direction of many campaigns for major offices is placed in the hands of paid professional campaign managers or public-relations experts. Increasingly it is more accurate to refer to "candidate" or "officeholder" politics rather than to "party" politics.

Because the official party organizations tend to emphasize nominations and elections instead of issues, are often dominated by officeholders, and provide little opportunity for mass participation in party affairs, various extralegal party organizations have been established. Both parties have created women's organizations and youth organizations. In addition, club-style unofficial organizations have sprung up, particularly in California, New York, and Wisconsin. These clubs have been formed primarily by well-educated upper-middle-class persons, who are interested in ideological issues but who usually do not want to hold public office.

Interparty Competition in States. Political scientists have devoted considerable research to competition between the parties at the state and local levels. Researchers have presented somewhat different conclusions, however, depending on the time-span covered in their analyses and the particular offices included. For example, scholars who have focused entirely on the election of state officials have produced slightly different results from those who have also surveyed presidential and congressional elections.

Despite these differences, there is general agreement that the state party systems may be classified on the basis of interparty competition as two-party, modified one-party, and one-party. As indicated in Table 1–2, the party systems of only approximately half of the states resemble the national party system from the standpoint of party competition. In several other states there is fairly even competition between the two parties for presidential electoral votes, Senate seats, and the governorship, but one party customarily wins most other offices. In a number of modified one-party states one party predominates, but the other party may receive as much as one-third of the votes and will elect a few candidates. The remaining one-sixth of the states, all in the South, have been classified as one-party states, for—except in presidential elections—the opposing party seldom provides serious competition for the party in power. In some of these one-party states, the second party may even fail to nominate candidates for most local and congressional positions. One point should be noted regarding the state party systems: while there are constant changes in the pattern of competition, the over-all trend appears to be toward more interparty competition. In particular, a political transformation seems to be occurring in the South; and if the Republicans continue to make gains in that area, there may soon be no one-party states.

Why do not all states have competitive two-party systems? Apparently the basic prerequisite for a two-party system is the existence of competing

TABLE 1–2. *The Fifty States Classified According to Degree of Interparty Competition*

One-Party Democratic	Modified One-Party Democratic	Two-Party		Modified One-Party Republican
South Carolina	Virginia	Alaska	Pennsylvania	Wisconsin
Georgia	North Carolina	Missouri	California	New Hampshire
Louisiana	Tennessee	Rhode Island	Nebraska	Iowa
Mississippi	Oklahoma	Washington	Illinois	Kansas
Texas	Kentucky	Delaware	Idaho	Maine
Alabama	Arizona	Nevada	Michigan	South Dakota
Arkansas	West Virginia	Massachusetts	New Jersey	North Dakota
Florida	Maryland	Hawaii	Indiana	Vermont
	New Mexico	Colorado	Oregon	
		Montana	Ohio	
		Minnesota	Wyoming	
		Utah	New York	
		Connecticut		

Adapted from Austin Ranney, "Parties in State Politics," in Herbert Jacob and Kenneth Vines (eds.), *Politics in the American States*, Boston: Little, Brown, 1965, p. 65. This table is based on partisan control of state elective offices during 1946–1963.

complexes of social and economic interests. In the one-party South and the modified one-party states there tends to be one dominant interest, or at least an absence of two or more strong and well-organized interests, or networks of interests. One-partyism in the South is largely a result of the efforts of the white southerners to limit the political activities of the Blacks.

In a number of the two-party states—such as New York, Pennsylvania, Ohio, and Illinois—the voters tend to be politically divided according to rural and urban areas and according to their social and economic status. In such states the Republicans are usually predominant in rural areas, the small towns, and among the more affluent urban and suburban groups and the Democrats among urban laborers, ethnic and religious minorities, and, in general, lower-income groups. As the individual states become more economically diversified and urbanized, their populations tend to be more heterogeneous, and competing complexes of interests may be expected to develop. Hence, the long-term trend is for greater interparty competition within the states, a trend already noticeable throughout much of the nation and especially in the South.

Municipal Politics

In the United States there are more than 18,000 municipalities, ranging in size from incorporated towns with less than a hundred persons to New York City with a population of over 8 million. The politics of these varied municipalities are affected by many factors which influence the politics of the state. The tremendous variety of cities obviously makes generalizing about municipal politics difficult and not entirely satisfactory.

Political Trends in Cities. Although cities vary greatly, the following political trends are discernible in municipalities across the nation. First, in many cities one party consistently dominates the political scene. This is not to say that the same party typically controls all urban governments in a given area. Instead, as is commonly known, the Democrats have majorities in most large and medium-size cities, whereas outside the South, the smaller cities, towns, and suburbs are typically Republican. Second, in a few cities the two major parties compete on fairly even terms. Examples of cities with interparty competition are Philadelphia, Cincinnati, and Indianapolis. Third, although in the past many cities were run by party bosses and machines, today municipalities with political bosses and well-organized political machines are virtually nonexistent. The best-known machine-controlled city today is Chicago, under Major Richard Daley. Fourth, there has been a general decline in the influence of party organizations in municipal politics. In some cities the parties are so disorganized or so split by factionalism that they wield very little power. In many cities campaigns for public office commonly emphasize the personalities of the candidates and their group associations more than their party affiliations or the relevant issues. Fifth, during recent decades there has been a constant increase in the proportion of cities employing nonpartisan nominations and elections. Of cities with 5,000 population or more the number using the nonpartisan system increased from 56 percent in 1940 to 65 percent in 1968.[5] A considerable part of the increase is apparently due to the adoption of the manager-council form of municipal government which often is linked with nonpartisan elections.

Nonpartisan Politics. In most nonpartisan cities the nonpartisan primary is in effect the first stage of an election. If a person receives more than 50 percent of the votes cast for an office, he is declared to be elected without running in the general election. If no candidate receives a majority of the votes, the two candidates for each office receiving the most

[5] *The Municipal Year Book, 1968*, Washington, D.C.: International City Manager's Association, 1968, p. 58.

votes are the nominees, and their names appear on the general election ballot. Some cities use nonpartisan elections without a primary; names of candidates are placed on the ballot by petition, and the candidate receiving a plurality of votes is elected, even though he might not have had a majority of the votes.

The two principal arguments for nonpartisan elections are that (1) better officials are obtained, and (2) party politics should be removed from local government. On the first point, advocates of nonpartisanship have asserted that some people will run for office who would not do so under a partisan label, and that voters will cast their ballots for the "best" man and not the party. It is impossible to prove objectively whether partisan or nonpartisan elections produce the more able candidates; however, students of municipal governments have generally concluded that changing from a partisan to a nonpartisan system has not changed dramatically the caliber of local officials.

Regarding the elimination of party politics from local government, the experience of cities which have adopted nonpartisan systems reveals several types of political patterns. In some municipalities the political parties are merely transformed from formal legal involvement to informal and extra-legal involvement in elections. For instance, Chicago has nonpartisan elections, but Richard Daley and his Democratic organization have controlled the city by winning elections. In other cities one or both parties have joined civic associations to support candidates. But in a number of nonpartisan cities the parties have not openly been involved in local campaigns; they have supported candidates either secretly or not at all. Duane Lockard has summarized the experience of nonpartisan cities as follows: "if by removal of 'politics' from local government we mean the removal of the party from an effective role in local elections, it appears true that adoption of the system often eliminates the parties. In varying degrees they may covertly—or, in some cases, openly—participate, but the scattered and not very conclusive evidence available suggests that parties are usually reduced to minimal roles."[6]

Critics have asserted that nonpartisan elections diminish the role of political parties, increase the influence of the press and certain special interest groups in elections, and tend to benefit the incumbents and the more conservative candidates. A study made in California, where all local officials are elected on nonpartisan ballots, indicates that more Republicans than Democrats have been elected to nonpartisan offices. Although registered Democrats in California outnumbered registered Republicans by a ratio of three to two, in twenty-six cities with more than 50,000 pop-

[6] Lockard, op. cit., p. 218.

ulation 68 percent of the council members and 80 percent of the mayors are registered Republicans.[7]

Community Political Power

Abraham Lincoln's frequently quoted phrase, "Government of the people, by the people, and for the people," explains very little regarding how public policies are actually formulated and adopted. In the modern political world what does government "by the people" mean? Basically, who makes the important political decisions—all the people, a majority, or only the political activists? If the activists have disproportionate influence, is political power dispersed with different groups wielding authority in particular areas, or does a small élite make most of the major decisions?

In an effort to obtain answers to such questions, social scientists have made a number of detailed investigations of politics in local communities. This attention to community politics is in part due to the realization that the local communities may be microcosms of the complexes of social and political interests found at the state and national levels of government, and that by analyzing local political communities insights may be gained concerning the larger political systems. Thus, the study of community power structures, i.e., who makes the authoritative political decisions in the community, may advance our understanding of the political process on the state and national scenes.

The Power Élite Model. The studies of politics in communities have produced two competing explanations of local political authority. These are commonly referred to as the "power élite" and the "pluralist" models. Advocates of the power-élite approach contend that political power in a community is concentrated in a small cohesive élite drawn from the top socioeconomic class, usually the principal business and financial leaders. Although most protagonists of this proposition have limited their analysis to individual cities, some have extended its application to larger communities, including the entire nation.[8]

Élitist analyses of local communities began in the 1920s, but the current interest in community power structures generally dates from sociologist Floyd Hunter's study of Atlanta, Georgia, published in 1953 under the title, *Community Power Structure: A Study of Decision Makers.* In Atlanta "the test for admission to the circle of decision makers," Hunter maintained, was "almost wholly a man's position in the business commu-

[7] Eugene C. Lee, *The Politics of Nonpartisanship,* Berkeley: University of California Press, 1960, pp. 56–57.

[8] See C. Wright Mills, *The Power Élite,* New York, Oxford University Press, 1956.

nity."[9] According to him, community power might be depicted as a pyramidal structure headed by a clique of top business leaders with lower-ranking élites composed of civic, professional, religious, and educational leaders and the elected public officials. The top élite, Hunter asserted, made the important community decisions and passed them down to the lower-level leaders and to the public officials for implementation. The rank-and-file citizens of the community exercised very little direct or indirect political influence or power.

In brief, proponents of the power-élite approach have generally maintained that local communities are governed almost exclusively by a relatively permanent, single élite group, which is not representative of the community, but whose power and influence include the ability to make decisions concerning most important community issues. Although some disagreement may occur within the élite, the members share the same basic attitudes and have a commonality of interests. The formal political leaders and officeholders are seen as subservient to the élite, the actual rulers of the community.

The Pluralist Model. Following the publication of Hunter's study, a number of political scientists conducted research in the power relationships in cities ranging in size from New York City down to relatively small communities. From these investigations a pluralist model of community power has been constructed which differs sharply from the power-élite approach. Of these studies Robert Dahl's analysis of decision-making in New Haven has been the most influential.[10]

Like the élitist scholars, advocates of the pluralist model found that only a small proportion of the population was politically active. Dahl noted that "the political system of New Haven is characterized by the presence of two sharply contrasting groups of citizens. The great body of citizens use their political resources at a low level; a tiny body of professionals use their political resources at a high level."[11] Proponents of the pluralist approach assert, however, that the communities they observed are not dominated by a small homogeneous ruling clique. For instance, Wallace Sayre and Herbert Kaufman state categorically that "no single ruling élite dominates the political and governmental system of New York City."[12]

---

[9] Floyd Hunter, *Community Power Structure: A Study of Decision Makers,* Chapel Hill: University of North Carolina Press, 1953, p. 79.

[10] Robert A. Dahl, *Who Governs?* New Haven: Yale University Press, 1961.

[11] *Ibid.,* p. 305.

[12] Wallace S. Sayre and Herbert Kaufman, *Governing New York City,* New York: Norton, 1965, p. 710.

Instead of a monolithic power structure, the pluralists believe that political power tends to be dispersed among a variety of persons and groups and that persons who are influential in one issue-area may exert little power in other areas. Dahl writes: "Probably the most striking characteristic of influence in New Haven is the extent to which it is specialized; that is, individuals who are influential in one sector of public activity tend not to be influential in another sector. . . ."[13]

A detailed analysis of political decision-making in Syracuse resulted in similar conclusions: "First, the myth that significant decisions in Syracuse emanate from one source does not stand up under close scrutiny. Second, there tend to be as many decision centers as there are important decision areas, which means that the decision-making power is fragmented among the institutions, agencies, and individuals which cluster about these areas. Third, in reality there appear to be many kinds of community power. . . ."[14] A few years after Hunter's study of Atlanta, M. Kent Jennings making a second study of that city found three kinds of decision-makers and concluded that of the three types the "economic dominants" —the top business and financial leaders—were least influential in political decision-making.[15]

Exponents of the pluralist model of community power have thus generally agreed that political activists exercise disproportionate power, but that the community is not governed by a cohesive ruling élite. Instead there are multiple centers of power made up of elected public officials and private persons and groups. Power relationships are not highly structured and permanent but are subject to change with different leadership groups exerting influence on different issues. The power of most groups is limited by the countervailing power of others. In such a political environment there is a high probability that most interested persons and groups may participate effectively in the decision-making process, and the extent to which a person takes part in political decisions is determined largely by his own interest.

What accounts for these two opposing interpretations of community power? In part the answer may be found in the different research designs and methods of the two groups of social scientists. The élitists, who are mostly sociologists, have generally used "reputational" analysis, which involves interviewing community residents to obtain names of persons considered to be influential, and from these initial listings determining

13 Dahl, op. cit., p. 169.

14 Roscoe C. Martin, Decisions in Syracuse, Bloomington, Ind.: Indiana University Press, 1961, p. 311.

15 M. Kent Jennings, Community Influentials: The Elites of Atlanta, New York: Free Press, 1964, pp. 193–205.

through further interviews and analysis the real wielders of power. Critics contend that the élitists incorrectly equate social status, wealth, and leadership in the business community with political power, and that they assume the existence of a monolithic structure of authority in a community which they prove to their own satisfaction by using the "reputational" approach.

The pluralists in general reject both the results and the methodology of the élitists. They have usually proceeded by delineating different "issue-areas" and then analyzing which people or groups have direct influence on decisions in those areas. Although there have been some critics of this approach, most political scientists accept the pluralist analysis of political power. In actuality, the degree to which political power is concentrated undoubtedly varies considerably from one community to another and depends primarily on the number of organized social and economic interests and the effectiveness with which those interests promote their particular goals.

chapter 2
THE LEGISLATIVE
PROCESS IN
THE STATES

All fifty states, like the national government, have the tripartite division of governmental powers—legislative, executive, and judicial. State constitutions vest the legislative power primarily in the state legislatures, whose principal function is the determination of public policy through the enactment of law. Through the enactment of statutory measures the legislature decides what the state government will do, the nature of the agencies that will perform the various activities, and the amount of money to be spent by each agency; it also determines how the money is to be raised. All lawmaking functions, however, are not confined to the state legislature. The governor as a policy formulator has become a chief legislator; many administrative agencies may promulgate rules and regulations that have the force of law; and even the courts help establish public policy. Moreover, in a number of states the voters may directly enact and repeal legislation through the initiative and referendum.

POWERS OF STATE LEGISLATURES

Although the primary function of the legislatures is the formulation of public policy through the enactment of statutory law, state legislatures possess other important powers. Thus the powers of state legislatures may be classified into two general categories: (1) legislative, or lawmaking, and (2) non-lawmaking.

23

Legislative Powers

Under the American constitutional system, each state possesses all powers of government that are not prohibited to it by the national Constitution, laws, or treaties, or by its own constitution. Consequently, the states are not limited to the powers expressly granted by their constitutions, but have inherent powers of government. Hence a state legislature, in addition to enacting legislation directly authorized by its state constitution, may pass laws on many subjects not specifically mentioned in that document. The state lawmaking power is therefore a combination of inherent powers and specific constitutional authority. It includes the following:

First, the legislatures establish all governmental departments and agencies not provided by the state constitution.

Second, the legislature controls the public purse. Although the governor is expected to take the lead in preparing the budget, the legislature approves the budget, and it has the authority to levy taxes, borrow money, and appropriate funds.

Third, the legislature enacts the statutes that provide for the organization and authority of governing agencies in cities, counties, and other local government units. Although cities and counties in a number of states have been granted considerable autonomy, the state legislatures still have much responsibility for government at the local level.

Fourth, the state legislatures enact a wide variety of laws which have a direct impact on the lives of the citizenry. Among these are laws relating to marriage and divorce, private property, corporations, deeds, mortgages, contracts, and laws protecting the people by specifying and defining the punishment of various crimes. Of primary importance are the laws enacted under the states' police power—laws to protect the safety, health, morals, convenience, order, and general welfare of the people. The police power vests the state legislatures with the broadest inherent and residual authority that it possesses. Examples of legislation based on police power may be seen in the laws pertaining to health and working conditions; laws requiring the licensing and regulating of various professions, industries, and trades; laws regulating the production and sale of intoxicating liquors and explosives; and laws authorizing cities and counties to enact ordinances relating to sanitation, health, zoning, traffic, and other matters.

Non-lawmaking Powers

No fewer than five types of activity other than lawmaking occupy some of the time of one or both houses of state legislatures.

Constituent Powers. As has been explained previously, legislatures are authorized to propose constitutional amendments and to submit to the voters the question of calling a constitutional convention. When the legislature participates in changing the constitution, it exercises what is known as the constituent power.

Executive Functions. In most states many of the appointments made by the governor to administrative posts, boards, and commissions, and, in some states, to the judiciary, must be approved by the senate. In approving these appointments the senate is performing an executive function that dates back to the colonial days when the upper house served as an executive council to the governor. In certain southern and New England states the legislature elects some of the judges and administrative officials. For example, in New Hampshire the legislature elects the treasurer and the secretary of state.

Administrative Powers. Although the governor has the primary responsibility for directing and supervising the administration, the legislature has some administrative powers. In addition to creating administrative agencies, defining their tasks, and appropriating funds for their support, the legislature may specify their procedures and organization. In the early history of the United States much legislation was self-executing in that the legislature enacted laws and left the enforcement to individuals who brought action in courts against offenders. As life in the United States has grown more complex and the activities of government have proliferated, legislatures have created administrative agencies to enforce public policies and have delegated quasi-legislative (rule-making) powers to them. An increasing proportion of administrative law is therefore promulgated by administrative officials. The legislatures, however, retain the responsibility for ensuring that the intent and purposes of the legislature are carried out, and investigations provide one means for doing so.

Investigatory Powers. The power to investigate inheres in the state legislatures—as well as in Congress—as an essential adjunct to their other powers. Often investigations are conducted to gain information regarding suspected mismanagement, corruption, or inefficiency in an executive department or agency. Investigations are also conducted to explore areas in which new legislation may be required. These inquiries are often started by the adoption of a resolution providing for a committee of a single house or a joint committee to investigate some topic or problem.

Judicial Powers. State legislatures, like Congress, possess limited judicial powers. They can decide whether to seat a member whose election and right to take office are questioned. They may also pass judgment on a member who has been accused of misconduct and may expel him. Legislatures also customarily have the power to impeach state elective officers and judges. The procedure in impeachment cases is similar to that prescribed for members of Congress. Typically, to initiate a case a resolution of impeachment must be adopted in the lower house and then the upper house tries the case.

LEGISLATIVE STRUCTURE

Bicameralism and Unicameralism

After the Revolutionary War all states established bicameral systems, primarily because of the precedent of the two houses of Congress and the British Parliament. This pattern was continued by all states until 1937, when Nebraska adopted a unicameral legislature.

The relative advantages of bicameral and unicameral systems have been widely discussed in the United States. Those who support the bicameral plan argue that it permits better representation for all segments of the citizenry and that each of the two houses provides a check on ill-considered or hasty action by the other house. Proponents of unicameralism assert that the two-house system obscures responsibility for legislative actions and encourages deadlocks. They argue that a unicameral system would be more efficient and economical and that it would result in increased prestige and pay for the smaller number of legislators and for that reason would induce better-qualified individuals to run for the legislature. They believe that the unicameral plan has been successful in Nebraska, and that it might work as well in other states. Although the model state constitution of the National Municipal League provides for a unicameral legislature, there appears relatively little interest in it among the general electorate, outside of Nebraska, and at this time it appears unlikely that other states will soon adopt a unicameral system.

Names and Sizes of Legislative Bodies

State legislatures are called by different names. A majority of the states call their lawmaking bodies the *Legislature*; in nearly two-fifths of the states they are called the *General Assembly*; in three states, the *Legislative Assembly*; and in Massachusetts and New Hampshire the legislature is referred to as the *General Court*. In all states the upper house is called the *Senate*, but a variety of names are applied to the lower house, including

House of Representatives (which is most commonly used), the *Assembly*, the *General Assembly*, or the *House of Delegates*.

The principal differences in the two houses of state legislatures are in their size and the length of terms of members. The senates are invariably smaller in size; and because the same electorate chooses the members of both houses, the constituencies of the senators are usually somewhat larger than those of lower house members. In approximately three-quarters of the states, senators are elected for four-year terms, while in all but four states the lower house members are elected for two years. States electing senators for four years usually stagger the terms and elect half of them every two years. The smaller membership and longer terms of senators add to their prestige and influence, hence membership in the upper houses is generally considered more desirable than in the lower house.

The size of each house is determined by the state constitutions in some states, while in others the constitution fixes certain limitations and permits legislators to establish the exact number. Nebraska's unicameral legislature has 49 members. Lower houses range in size from 39 in Delaware to 400 in New Hampshire; however, most lower houses vary in size from 75 to 150. Several of the larger houses are in New England, where the town is the unit of representation. State senates are considerably smaller than lower houses and vary in size from 20 in Alaska and Nevada to 67 in Minnesota. The two largest states in population, California and New York, have 40 and 57, respectively, in their senates and 80 and 150 in their lower houses. (See Table 2–1.)

Basis of Representation

The size and basis of representation of each house in state legislatures have been largely the result of compromises made at the time state constitutions have been drafted. A number of states have provided for representation in one house on the basis of population and in the other on the basis of governmental jurisdictions, usually counties (towns in New England), regardless of the disparities in the size of such jurisdictions. Constitutions have commonly provided that in at least one house each county have a minimum of one representative, that no county have more than a certain proportion of seats regardless of its population, or that in one house each county be given equal representation. As a result of such provisions, in virtually every state the growing urban and suburban areas have been underrepresented and the sparsely populated areas overrepresented in the state legislatures. For example, in 1960 Cook County, Illinois, had over half of the state's population but only 24 of the 58 state senators. Los

TABLE 2–1. *State Legislatures*

State	Upper House Size	Upper House Years	Lower House Size	Lower House Years	Regular Sessions
Alabama	35	4	106	4	Biennial
Alaska	20	4	40	2	Annual
Arizona	30	2	60	2	"
Arkansas	35	4	100	2	Biennial
California	40	4	80	2	Annual
Colorado	34	4	65	2	"
Connecticut	36	2	177	2	Biennial
Delaware	19	4	39	2	Annual
Florida	48	4	117	2	Biennial
Georgia	56	2	195	2	Annual
Hawaii	25	4	51	2	"
Idaho	35	2	70	2	Biennial
Illinois	58	4	177	2	"
Indiana	50	4	100	2	"
Iowa	61	4	124	2	"
Kansas	40	4	125	2	Annual
Kentucky	38	4	100	2	Biennial
Louisiana	39	4	105	4	Annual
Maine	32	2	151	2	Biennial
Maryland	43	4	142	4	Annual
Massachusetts	40	2	240	2	"
Michigan	38	4	110	2	"
Minnesota	67	4	135	2	Biennial
Mississippi	52	4	132	4	"
Missouri	34	4	163	2	"
Montana	55	4	104	2	"
Nebraska	49	4	—	—	"
Nevada	20	4	40	2	"
New Hampshire	24	2	400	2	"
New Jersey	40	4	80	2	Annual
New Mexico	42	4	70	2	"
New York	57	2	150	2	"
North Carolina	50	2	120	2	Biennial
North Dakota	49	4	98	2	"
Ohio	33	4	99	2	"
Oklahoma	48	4	99	2	"
Oregon	30	4	60	2	"
Pennsylvania	50	4	203	2	Annual
Rhode Island	50	2	100	2	"
South Carolina	46	4	124	2	"

TABLE 2–1. *State Legislatures* (Continued)

| State | Upper House | | Lower House | | Regular |
	Size	Years	Size	Years	Sessions
South Dakota	35	2	75	2	,,
Tennessee	33	2	99	2	Biennial
Texas	31	4	150	2	,,
Utah	28	4	69	2	,,
Vermont	30	2	150	2	,,
Virginia	40	4	100	2	,,
Washington	49	4	99	2	,,
West Virginia	34	4	100	2	Annual
Wisconsin	33	4	100	2	Biennial
Wyoming	30	4	61	2	,,

SOURCES: "Elective Offices of State and Local Governments," *Census of Governments,* 1967, Washington, D.C.: U.S. Department of the Census, 1967; and *Taylor's Encyclopedia of Government Officials,* Dallas, Texas: Political Research, Inc., 1969.

Angeles County had 38 percent of California's population but chose only 1 of the 40 state senators.

The arguments most often heard for such systems of representation are that they are similar to our federal government and that each house should be based on different systems of representation. Those who have opposed disproportionate representation have argued that each person's vote should count the same in electing representatives, and that the federal and state legislatures are not analogous. In regard to the latter point they noted that the system of representation in Congress was instituted because of the historical necessity of compromising between the demands of the large and small states, and within our federal system the states are political units that have considerable autonomy and exercise powers granted them by the federal Constitution, whereas the counties are administrative subdivisions of the states and exercise only those powers granted them by the states.

Reapportionment

Unequal representation of urban and suburban areas in state legislatures has been due not only to the basis of representation but also to the failure of the state legislature to reapportion legislative districts. Although state constitutions customarily provide for reapportioning of legislative districts after each federal census, in 1962, 27 state legislatures had not been reapportioned within the preceding 25 years and some for much longer. The legislature of Alabama had not been reapportioned since 1901, Minnesota since 1913, and Mississippi since 1916.

Partly because of the failure of legislatures to reapportion the districts, some states have granted other agencies the responsibility for adjusting districts to population movements and growth. The two newest states, Alaska and Hawaii, have authorized the governor, with the assistance of an advisory commission, to reapportion the legislature. Missouri, in its 1945 constitution, established a commission, appointed by the governor from lists submitted by party officials, to redistrict the state senate, and empowered the secretary of state to reapportion its lower house on the basis of a prescribed formula. Other states, including Texas, South Dakota, Ohio, and California, have provided for boards to reapportion their states if their legislatures fail to act.

On various occasions efforts have been made to seek judicial action to force a reapportionment of legislative districts, but prior to 1962 the courts declined to accept jurisdiction. In that year the United States Supreme Court ruled in the case of *Baker* v. *Carr* that the equal protection clause of the federal Constitution could be invoked to test the fairness of representation in a state legislature. This case involved Tennessee, which had refused to reapportion since 1901 despite shifts in the population. Shortly after this decision several states reapportioned on a population basis, and cases involving legislative apportionment in other states were taken to the courts. Later, in 1964, the federal Supreme Court elaborated on the earlier decision by ruling in *Reynolds* v. *Sims* that both houses of state legislatures must be apportioned on a population basis and that "the Equal Protection Clause requires that a state make an honest and good faith effort to construct districts in both houses of its legislature, as nearly of equal population as is practicable." Thus the Court established the principle of "one man, one vote" for both houses of state legislatures.

Qualifications and Compensations of Legislators

All state constitutions set forth certain qualifications for legislators. Typically they must be over a certain age, citizens, residents of the state and district for a stated length of time, and registered or qualified voters. Each house is the judge of the qualifications and election of its members.

Formerly most states established the salaries of the legislators in their constitutions and it was usually difficult to obtain amendments granting salary increases or permitting the legislators to determine their salaries. Until the end of World War II most states allowed their legislators only a small per diem payment and that for a limited number of days. Now nearly three-quarters of the states pay annual salaries and a number permit the legislators—like the members of Congress—to establish their own salaries. In addition to the salaries, some states provide per diem and mileage allowances and payments into a pension fund. Even with the increased payments only a few of the larger states—such as California, Illinois, Massachusetts, Michigan, New York, Pennsylvania, and Wisconsin—provide an adequate income for their legislators. In 1967 compensation for a biennium for a typical legislator in salary and other allowances ranged from $200 in New Hampshire to $24,000 in Pennsylvania and New York and $25,000 in Michigan.

The Legislators

A recent survey of the legislators of one of the larger states revealed that the typical legislator of that state is a college graduate, a member of a number of civic and service organizations, and is usually well known in his community. If he is a senator, he is about 52 years of age; if he is a member of the lower house, he is about 48. The great majority of legislators are from the fields of business and law. This, of course, is to be expected, for persons in these occupations are often active in civic affairs and are more likely than most others to be able to take time from their employment to campaign for office and, if elected, to perform the duties of the office while continuing their former occupations on a part-time basis. Although legislators' salaries have generally been increased in recent years, they are still not sufficient in most states to attract many well-qualified persons who do not have another source of income.

Sessions

In the early history of the country most legislatures met annually. Usually no limitations were placed on the length of sessions, but because the problems then confronting the states were not highly complicated most sessions were short. During the nineteenth century dissatisfaction developed regarding state legislatures; and, partly for that reason, by the beginning of the twentieth century most states had adopted biennial sessions and limited the number of days the legislators could meet. In recent years there has been a trend back toward annual sessions. In 1940 only four states held annual sessions, but by the 1960s more than twenty states were holding annual regular sessions.

Most of the large industrial states, including New York, Michigan, Massachusetts, and California, now hold annual legislative sessions. Some of these states hold general legislative sessions every second year and sessions limited to consideration of the budget in alternate years. In states in which budgetary sessions are held, it is not uncommon for the governor to call a special session to run concurrently with the budget session. This, in effect, permits a limited general session to be held at the same time as the budgetary session.

In all states special legislative sessions may also be called by the governor, and in a few states by members of the legislature. In a majority of the states, during special sessions the legislature may consider only the subject or subjects specified by the governor when calling the special session.

Many students of government believe that most, if not all, states should establish annual legislative sessions and that no limitation should be placed on the length of such sessions. They reason that in these rapidly changing times annual sessions are required to provide adequate consideration for the numerous complex and pressing problems that devolve upon state legislatures. They also argue that sessions of limited duration are partly responsible for many of the "bad" state laws. A committee of the American Political Science Association reported that because of the restrictions on the duration of sessions "a strong minority may thwart the interest of the majority through delaying tactics. Bills piled up at the end of the session are rushed through without adequate consideration. . . . Restrictions on length of sessions are the real reasons for bad laws. . . ."[1]

Opponents of annual sessions of unlimited duration have opposed proposals establishing such sessions on the grounds that they would be more expensive and would tend to eliminate persons who wish to continue in their occupations while serving as legislators. In one state considering unlimited sessions an argument against the proposal was that "the people have the right to know when the legislature would adjourn." This argument is often heard from special interest groups who retain lobbyists in state capitols during legislative sessions.

ORGANIZATION OF THE LEGISLATURE

Officers

The organization and functioning of state legislatures are similar to that of Congress. The presiding officer of the lower house in every state is the speaker, who is often more powerful relatively than his counterpart in Congress. Customarily his powers include appointing the members of all committees of his house, referring bills to committees, recognizing members who wish to speak, and exercising various other powers as presiding officer—such as putting questions to a vote, keeping order, interpreting the rules and deciding points of order and signing all acts, resolutions, war-

[1] Belle Zeller, ed., *American State Legislatures*, New York: Thomas Y. Crowell, 1954, p. 93.

rants, and other documents ordered by his house. In states in which the Rules Committee exercises broad powers, he is often its chairman. Because of his powers, the speaker is often the most important single individual in the state legislature and, except for the governor, the most influential official in the state.

In a majority of the states the lieutenant governor, who is popularly elected, presides over the senate. Like the Vice-President, his counterpart in the United States Senate, he usually has few powers other than recognizing members who desire the floor, deciding on points of order, and voting in case of a tie vote in the senate. In the twelve states that do not have a lieutenant governor, the senate elects its presiding officer. In any event, the senate usually elects a president or a president pro tempore, who often possesses broad powers, including the authority to appoint members of senate committees. However, in about one-fifth of the states committee members are appointed by a committee selected for that purpose.

Committees

State legislatures, like Congress, make extensive use of committees. The most important committees are the standing committees, which function during the sessions and are usually re-established each time a general session convenes. Bills and resolutions are customarily referred to a standing committee before being considered by either house as a body. The subject matter over which the standing committees are given jurisdiction cover all principal areas of state lawmaking—such as agriculture, education, and social welfare. In general, the state committees do not have as much influence over the content of legislation as do congressional committees.[2] Expertness in subject fields is more difficult to achieve on the state level because of the shorter and less frequent sessions, the high rate of turnover in legislative personnel, and inadequate staff assistance. Legislators are not necessarily reassigned to the same committee as is the custom in Congress. Furthermore, committee chairmanships do not always go to the senior party member or even to a member of the majority party in that house.

During the past two decades most state legislatures have followed the precedent set by Congress and have reduced the number of their standing committees. The average number of such committees is now twenty-two in lower houses and twenty in state senates. Many political observers believe that there are still too many committees. One reason for the large number of committees has been that additional legislators are thus permitted the added prestige of being committee chairmen. One disadvantage of a large

[2] In this regard, committees of American state legislatures resemble the committees in the British Parliament much more than congressional committees.

number of committees is that each legislator is required to serve on too many committees. A criticism often raised is that the work load of the committees is unevenly divided. Typically, several of the more important committees have large numbers of bills referred to them, whereas other committees receive relatively few.

Three states—Connecticut, Maine, and Massachusetts—use joint committees to handle most of their legislative business, and other states use joint committees to consider appropriations and revenue measures and occasionally for other purposes. With the membership thus being drawn from both houses, joint committees can often avoid the deadlocks and duplication of efforts that are characteristic of legislatures with separate sets of committees for each house.

Rules of Procedure

The procedure followed by legislatures in enacting law is governed by their state constitutions, government codes, and the rules adopted by the two houses. State constitutions, for example, generally establish the number of members that will constitute a quorum. Government codes usually contain provisions not included in the constitutions but which the legislators believe should be at least semipermanently fixed, such as prescriptions regarding what officers shall be elected in each house of the legislature. Within the limits of constitutional and statutory provisions, the legislature is free to determine its own rules of procedure.

The rules customarily govern such matters as the daily order of business, the number and membership of committees, and the procedure followed in enacting legislation. In general, the states follow congressional precedents on such matters. One of the striking features of state legislative procedure is the inadequacy of the records. Only a few states keep records of committee hearings or of the debates on the floor of either house. In the other states journals record the votes and actions taken on bills, but there is no other official record to guide researchers or the courts regarding the legislative process or the intent of the lawmakers.

Staff and Auxiliary Services

As the responsibilities and problems of the legislatures have grown more numerous and complicated, the states have attempted to improve the legislative process by providing the legislators with better facilities and additional staff assistance.

As in other areas of state government, however, progress has not been uniform and diversity characterizes the practice of the several states. Many states make no provision for offices for individual legislators and provide the standing committees and legislators virtually no technical assistance and only limited secretarial help. On the other hand, in California, where the legislature has more than 600 employees on its payrolls, the legislators have facilities and staffs nearly comparable to those of Congress. Each lawmaker is provided a handsome office in the capitol and an allowance for one in his district, and he may employ an administrative assistant and one or two secretaries. In addition, California standing committees are amply staffed with well-qualified assistants, many of whom are experts in the area of particular concern to the committee to which they are assigned.

Legislative Reference Service. Library and reference services have been provided by some states—Massachusetts, New York, and Wisconsin—since the turn of the century, and nearly all states now have some such service. In some states the agencies providing these services are handicapped by insufficient funds, but in many others valuable assistance is provided. The functions of these agencies include providing centralized information services, conducting research, and obtaining information for the legislators. It does this in part by assembling and making available to the legislators statutes, judicial decisions, administrative reports, and other materials on any subject on which the legislature might act.

In some states the same agency performs the function of statutory revision by conducting a continuous examination of the laws to determine which ones have been repealed by implication or have become outmoded or defective for other reasons. In a few states, at the start of each general session the agency with this responsibility submits a report to the legislature listing defective or obsolete statutes.

Bill-drafting Agencies. Virtually all states provide a bill-drafting service. In some states the agency providing library and reference services also performs the bill-drafting function; in others a separate office staffed largely by attorneys performs this service. The trend across the nation is to have these experts draft virtually all of the bills, resolutions, and constitutional amendments that are introduced in the legislature.

Legislative Councils. Kansas in 1933 established a legislative council, which is a type of legislative clearinghouse. Since that time more than forty other states have created similar agencies. Ideally, the council should operate on a continuing basis, coordinating the research and investigatory activities of the legislature and planning its work. The council should consider the wide range of problems confronting the legislature in the next session and make recommendations for solutions of the problems. The councils customarily have permanent staffs of research personnel. The Committee on American Legislatures of the American Political Science Association has recommended that a legislative council be composed of 10 or 12 members selected on a bipartisan basis from the two legislative houses. In actuality, councils range in size from 5 in South Carolina to 260 in Pennsylvania, where all members of the legislature serve as members. Some councils have been highly successful, but others, because of lack of funds or the opposition of legislators not appointed to the council, have failed to live up to the expectations of their sponsors.

Fiscal Review Agencies. State legislatures in recent years have created fiscal review agencies to provide a comprehensive analysis of proposed budgets, a continuous review of state revenues and expenditures, and post-audits of expenditures. A number of states have assigned to their legislative council the responsibility of budget analysis and continuous fiscal review, and nearly one-half of the states have created staff agencies responsible for conducting post-audits of records and accounts.

Political Parties and the Legislature

Legislators are elected as members of political parties in all states except Minnesota and Nebraska, where they are elected on nonpartisan ballots. The parts played by the parties in the organization and functioning of the legislatures vary widely among the fifty states. Among the factors generally important in determining the roles of political parties in a state legislature are the influence of political interest groups, the press, sectional and urban-rural cleavages, and the comparative strength of the two parties. Of these factors, no doubt the most important is the extent to which the two political parties compete for power within the state.

In approximately one-fifth of the states one party is sufficiently strong that the influence of the second party is negligible. In these states, party caucuses are seldom, if ever, held. Factions within the dominant party often organize and compete for power within the legislature much the same as the parties do in two-party states. In some states the factions are semipermanently organized, whereas in others the legislators may group and regroup from one session to the next.

In a second category of states—those often referred to as modified one-party—one party is sufficiently strong that it usually elects a majority of the state officials, but the second party may elect a sizable number of legislators. The roles of the parties in these states vary greatly. In some states both parties are well organized and active, but in others the parties are only loosely organized and play very little part in the functioning of the legislature.

In still other states, where the two parties compete on nearly even terms, the parties are more likely than elsewhere to play prominent parts in the state legislative process. But even in these states much variation is found. In some states the parties function much the same as they do in Congress. In states such as New York and Connecticut, where party discipline is strong, the parties appear to have more important roles than in Congress. But in other two-party states the parties have not been highly organized, and the influence of the parties on the legislative output is considerably less than in the national legislature. In brief, the more the two parties tend to be evenly matched, the greater the likelihood that the parties will play prominent roles in the legislature, but the relative strength of the two parties is not the only factor that determines their influence in the legislative process.

The Enactment of a Law

The procedure followed by the various state legislatures in enacting law differs slightly from state to state, but in general it follows the pattern used by Congress. In brief, the steps by which a bill becomes a law in state legislatures are (1) introduction, (2) committee consideration, (3) action by first house, (4) action by second house, (5) conference committee, if necessary, (6) action by the governor.

Introduction. In order to introduce a bill a legislator ordinarily need only sign his name to the proposal and deliver it, or have it delivered, to the desk of the clerk or secretary of his legislative chamber.

Bills introduced into the legislatures receive their initial impetus from one of three sources. First, bills are initiated by the legislators themselves or by legislative committees; in most states, however, a smaller proportion of bills have this source of origin than in Congress. Second, some of the more important bills may originate with the governor, and bills are proposed by other state and local government officials. Third, in most states the great majority of bills come from political interest groups and private citizens.

Committee Consideration. After a bill is formally introduced, it is referred to a committee. The difference between state and national practices is pronounced at this stage. State legislative committees are more likely than are congressional committees to hold closed hearings, or not to publicize the dates of open hearings. Even if bills are discussed in open hearings, in most states committees make their decisions in executive session. Moreover, state committee reports on bills seldom indicate the vote of the members. In only a few states are committee hearings printed, and in a number of states even committee reports on individual bills are not printed. Furthermore, state committee reports on bills seldom indicate the vote of the members. As in Congress, committee consideration of bills is undoubtedly the most important step in the state legislative process. It is at this time that the bills are carefully examined. The undesirable ones are eliminated, and thorough consideration is given to those that seem to have merit.

Action by the First House. When a committee reports favorably on a bill, it is placed on the calendar or file of that house. Like Congress, most state legislatures require that each bill be read three times before enactment, and, with certain exceptions, the readings usually must occur on three separate days. This requirement of three readings dates back to a time when printed copies of bills were not available to legislators and was designed to enable the legislators to become thoroughly cognizant of the content of bills before voting on them. As most states now provide printed copies of bills to the legislators, for each bill to be read in full before the entire membership of either house would serve no useful purpose and would merely take time needed for the essential work of the legislature. Consequently, the requirement that the bills be *read* is circumvented, and usually only the title of the bill or part of it is actually read. Most bills that are adopted receive relatively little debate on the floor of either house. What debate does occur usually takes place at the time of the second or third reading of the bill.

Action by Second House. Although identical bills are occasionally introduced in both houses and proceed through the houses at about the same time, more commonly, after a bill has been adopted by one house, it must be transmitted to the second house, where the same procedure is followed. If the second house passes the bill without change, it goes to the governor for his approval. If the second house amends the bill, it then requests the first house to accept the amendment. Should the first house approve the amended bill, it is then enrolled and sent to the governor. But if the first house refuses the amendment, the bill is referred to a conference committee.

Conference Committees. Theoretically, the purpose of a conference committee is to compromise the two different versions of a bill. However, in a number of states conference committees are permitted to hold a "free conference," which means that the committee is not limited to those items of disagreement between the two houses, but may write new sections into the bill. Often conference committees hold several meetings, and much informal bargaining takes place before the committee members are able to agree. After the conference committee files its report, a majority vote in each house is necessary to approve the conference report. In most instances both houses approve conference reports. However, if either house refuses to accept the conference report, another conference committee may be appointed.

Action by the Governor. After a bill has been approved by both houses, it is sent to the governor, who usually may take any of several courses of action. He may sign the bill in which case it becomes a law. If he does not act within a given number of days and the legislature is in session, the bill becomes a law without his signature. In all states except North Carolina the governor may veto the bill, but his veto may be overruled by the legislature. As will be explained in Chapter 3, three-quarters of the states permit the governor to veto items of appropriation bills, and in slightly less than a third of the states the governor may pocket veto bills.

POLITICAL INTEREST GROUPS AND STATE LEGISLATURES

The influence of political interest groups on state legislatures varies considerably from one state to another. Based on information obtained in a survey conducted by the Committee on American Legislatures of the American Political Science Association, the states have been grouped into three categories, depending on whether the influence of political interest groups on the legislatures was considered to be strong, moderate, or weak. Of the forty-five states included in the survey, the influence of interest groups was considered strong in more than half of the states, moderate in nearly a third of the states, and weak in approximately a ninth of them. In general, political interest groups were considered strongest in states that were less wealthy, less industrial, and less urban, and those that were either one-party states or in which the political parties played only a minor role in the legislature.[3]

Political Interest Groups Classified

Primarily because of the great variety of political interest groups that lobby at the state capitols, no entirely satisfactory classification of such groups

[3] Harmon Zeigler, "Interest Groups in the States," in Herbert Jacob and Kenneth N. Vines (eds.), *Politics in the American States,* Boston: Little, Brown and Company, 1965, pp. 114–115.

has been developed. However, most of the political interest groups active at the state capitols may be placed in one of three categories.

First, there are a variety of groups, most of which are not highly active in lobbying, that are interested in legislation for other than economic reasons. These include such miscellaneous organizations as the Friends Committee on Legislation, the American Civil Liberties Union, and the League of Women Voters.

The second category consists of the semiofficial lobby composed of governmental agencies and organizations of public officials and employees. Included in this classification are state administrative departments and agencies, units of local government that send lobbyists to the capitol, organizations of state employees, and associations of state officials. The lobbying activities of these organizations and individuals are customarily related to obtaining legislation or appropriations that will further some state or local government program.

The third category comprises the heterogeneous nongovernmental associations, firms, and other groups that have an economic stake in the actions of the state legislature. Many of the major economic interests active in the national Capitol also have lobbyists in state capitols. By far the most numerous are the business groups; in the large industrial states one will usually find lobbying by a large variety of business associations, corporations, and individual firms. In such states there are, customarily, lobbyists employed by associations of retailers, manufacturers, bankers, railroads, truck lines, newspapers, insurance companies, the petroleum industry, real-estate brokers, and various other business interests. Also present in many state capitols are lobbyists representing organizations of workers, farmers, and leading professional groups—the legal, medical, and dental associations.

One means of appraising the influence of political interest groups is to ask state legislators which ones they consider to be most influential. Two groups of scholars have used this approach in investigating interest groups in states.[4] Business interests were generally considered the most powerful, followed by educational interests, organized labor, and farm groups. Due to particular circumstances within a state an organized interest may be politically influential there while not having influence in other states. Examples of such groups are trucking in North Carolina, insurance and horse-racing in Massachusetts, mining in Utah, and the lumber industry

[4] John C. Wahlke, Heinz Eulau, William Buchanan, and LeRoy C. Ferguson, *The Legislative System*, New York: Wiley, 1962; and Harmon Zeigler and Michael A. Baer, *Lobbying: Interaction and Influence in American State Legislatures*, Belmont, Calif.: Wadsworth, 1969. Zeigler and Baer asked lobbyists as well as legislators to name the organized interests they perceived as most powerful.

in Oregon.[5] A listing of the political interest groups considered most influential by the legislators of California, New Jersey, Ohio, and Tennessee is presented in Table 2–2.

Types and Methods of Lobbyists

There are two different types of lobbyists. First, there is the full-time employee or officer of a trade association or other group, who stays in the state capitol during legislative sessions and is involved in other activities for his employer during the other months of the year. Second, there are the lobbyists-for-hire, who may be employed by several associations, firms,

TABLE 2–2. *Interest Groups Considered Most Influential*
by Legislators of Four States

California	Ohio
(56 organizations named)	(68 organizations named)
California Teachers Association	Ohio Farm Bureau
AFL-CIO	Ohio Education Association
California Farm Bureau	Chamber of Commerce
California Medical Association	Ohio State Grange
League of California Cities	AFL-CIO
Chamber of Commerce	Ohio Manufacturer's Association
PTA(s)	Ohio Council of Retail Merchants
League of Women Voters	Ohio Medical Association
California State Grange	League of Women Voters
Legislative Committee	PTA(s)
California Taxpayers Association	
	Tennessee
New Jersey	(46 organizations named)
(38 organizations named)	Tennessee Education Association
New Jersey Education Association	Tennessee Municipal League
Chamber of Commerce	Tennessee Manufacturer's Association
AFL-CIO	Tennessee County Services Association
New Jersey Municipal League	tion
New Jersey Taxpayer Association	Tennessee Farm Bureau
New Jersey Manufacturer's Association	"Trading Stamps"
League of Women Voters	AFL-CIO
New Jersey Farm Bureau	Tennessee Taxpayers Association
PTA(s)	PTA(s)

SOURCE: John C. Wahlke, Heinz Eulau, William Buchanan, and LeRoy C. Ferguson, *The Legislative System*, New York: Wiley, 1962, pp. 318–319.

[5] Zeigler and Baer, *op. cit.*, pp. 31–34.

or other groups at the same time and who may change clients from one legislative session to the next. The former are usually more highly regarded and respected than the latter by the legislators and capitol reporters.

The most influential and active lobby groups are generally those with a direct economic interest in the work of the legislature. These groups, however, differ greatly in the extent of their interests and activity. Some groups are concerned with only a few bills and employ a lobbyist to represent them, or have their officers go to the state capitol only when bills of special interest to them are being considered. Other groups take stands on numerous legislative measures and are active in politics on virtually a year-round basis. Some such groups have one or more individuals permanently employed whose primary responsibility is to look after the political interests of that organization. During legislative sessions these persons are usually in the state capitol lobbying on bills; when the legislature is not in session, they often serve as attorneys, public-relations counselors, or executive directors for the organization.

The most important work of the lobbyists naturally occurs during legislative sessions. Bills incorporating desires of the group are drafted and given to legislators to be introduced. The lobbyists watch these bills as they proceed through the various phases of the legislative process to see that they are enacted in the form desired. As lobby groups also want to ensure that no legislation detrimental to their members is adopted, some organizations have their lobbyists and other staff members scrutinize every bill introduced to decide which they should oppose or attempt to have amended.

State lobbyists generally fall into three different categories. First, there is the *contact man* whose task is primarily to establish contact with individual legislators and, if possible, develop useful friendships. Second, there is the *informant* whose chief activity is to prepare information for presentation to legislators and committees. Third, there is the *watchdog* who reads every bill in order to inform his clients regarding the ones which might affect them.[6] These types are not mutually exclusive; however, most lobbyists view themselves as "contact" men or information brokers.

Some political interest groups have "stables" of legislators who cooperate with them either because they owe their election primarily to those groups or because they are themselves members of those groups. Interest associations with like-minded spokesmen in the legislature, or "inside lobbyists," naturally have advantages over other groups. Not uncommonly, the various lawyers, merchants, farmers, real-estate brokers, and others who are legislators join forces with specific lobbyists to work for their common cause. Lobbyists may rely on these legislators to guide their bills through

[6] *Ibid.*, p. 77.

to enactment; conversely, the legislators may seek the assistance of lobbyists in obtaining the support of other legislators for bills.

Political interest groups and their lobbyists do not limit their efforts to attempting to influence the legislators. After bills have been adopted by the legislature, they attempt to get the governor to approve or veto the measures. In states where the initiative and referendum are available, if a lobby group is unsuccessful in obtaining the desired action from the legislature and governor, it may use one of these two direct legislation devices.

DIRECT LEGISLATION

During the last half of the nineteenth century state and local legislative bodies were strongly criticized as being controlled and corrupted by special interest groups and political bosses. As a result, a number of reformers demanded the establishment of some form of "direct democracy" by which the people could directly determine public policy. In the years immediately preceding and following the turn of the century a number of states incorporated in their governmental systems the initiative and the referendum. These two governmental devices are tangible evidence of the Progressive movement that swept across the United States in those decades.

The Initiative

The initiative permits a specified number of voters to propose a statute or constitutional amendment by petition and to have it submitted to the voters for approval or rejection. Three kinds of initiatives are used in the several states: constitutional, direct statutory, and indirect statutory. In thirteen states the voters may propose amendments to the constitution through the initiative. In these and seven other states the voters may use the direct statutory initiative, and in five states the indirect statutory initiative is available. The procedures for obtaining the adoption of constitutional initiatives and direct statutory initiatives are identical. If the indirect initiative is used, a different procedure is followed.

Regardless of the form of the initiative, the first step is to draft the proposal and submit it to the secretary of state, who prepares a ballot title. Next the sponsors must obtain on the petition the number of signatures required by the state constitution—usually equal to 5, 8, or 10 percent of those voting in the preceding gubernatorial election. After the requisite number of signatures is obtained, if the constitutional initiative or direct statutory initiative is used, the proposal is placed on the ballot and is voted on in the next general election. Under the indirect form of initiative the proposition is presented to the legislature, which has the option of passing it without change or submitting it to the voters in the succeeding election. In some states, if the legislature declines to enact the measure, additional signatures must be obtained before it is submitted to the voters.

The Referendum

Several kinds of popular referendums are used at the state and local levels of government. As we have previously seen, a new state constitution and all constitutional amendments that originate in the legislatures must be approved by the voters. In addition, in most states bond issues, city and county charters, and amendments to such charters must be voted on by the electorate. However, strictly speaking, the term *referendum* does not apply to those instances. Instead, it is used only to refer to the petition or "protest" referendum, which is available only for statutes.

The petition referendum may be used by the people to require a measure enacted by the legislature to be submitted to the voters. Most legislation does not take effect until sixty or ninety days after being approved by the governor. If, during that time, a petition is signed by the requisite number of voters, the act does not become effective but must be referred to the electorate. In addition, in approximately half of the states using the referendum, the legislature may decide whether other measures that it has passed should be submitted to the voters. This is commonly referred to as the "optional" referendum.

Direct Legislation Appraised

At the time the initiative and referendum were first proposed they were the topics of considerable controversy, and even now differing opinions are held concerning their merits. Opponents of direct legislation have questioned the ability of thousands of voters in a state to reach intelligent decisions on complicated legislative measures, and they have expressed the fear that the initiative would result in the enactment of radical and impractical proposals. It is true that some initiative proposals have been long and technical and others have been unrealistic and unsound. Proponents of direct legislation cite the defeat of impractical plans as evidence that the electorate is capable of acting intelligently on direct legislative measures. On the other hand, critics express the opinion that the rejection of such proposals may be due largely to the fact that most people apparently follow the maxim of "when in doubt, vote 'no.'" Without question, one disadvantage of the initiative in some states has been the large amount of time and money required to defeat impractical plans.

For example, the voters in California, after defeating single-tax plans in four successive general elections, were confronted sixteen years later with a fifth single-tax plan, which they also rejected.

At the turn of the century the Progressive reformers argued that through direct legislation the people would be able to exercise more control over the legislative process and to reduce the influence of political interest groups. In several states the initiative has been used to enact a number of constructive proposals. Supporters have also expressed the belief that because the initiative is available, state legislatures have enacted measures that they might not otherwise have adopted. Others question this and assert that the legislative record of states like Washington and California, in which the initiative and referendum are available, is no more impressive than that of states like New York and Connecticut, in which the two direct legislation devices are not used.

The initiative and referendum obviously have not broken the power of pressure groups. Indeed, the great majority of initiative and referendum measures have originated with political interest groups. Relatively few citizen groups concerned with good government have the organization or the funds necessary to secure the signatures required to place a proposal on the ballot and to conduct a successful campaign. Because many special interest groups do have the money or workers, direct legislation, which was originally intended to curb the influence of pressure groups, has been used primarily by them. Despite the criticisms of direct legislation, few individuals in states where the initiative and referendum are employed would advocate their abandonment. In states where special interest groups are well organized and active, the initiative and refendum provide the electorate the means by which legislative decisions not in the general interest may be overruled.

LEGISLATIVE REFORMS

During recent years the functioning and reputation of state legislatures in general have markedly improved. Several factors have contributed to the increased effectiveness and status of the legislators. These include the reapportionment of legislative districts, the trend toward annual sessions, the reduction in the number of committees, additional staff services, and higher salaries for legislators which have added to the attractiveness of their positions. Although these reforms have not been uniformly adopted and all state legislatures have not shown pronounced improvement, more changes have occurred during the past few years than in any other comparable period.

Although the prestige and work of state legislatures have been enhanced, various other reforms are needed. Among the reforms that have been suggested are the following: Four-year terms for all legislators, a further reduction in the number of committees, more effective control and reporting of campaign contributions and expenditures, statutes that would provide adequate information regarding lobby groups and their lobbyists, and conflict-of-interest legislation that would prohibit lawmakers from engaging in any business or professional activity that might conflict with their responsibilities as state legislators. It is also apparent that state legislatures would be improved if legislators were more highly qualified. Many state legislators are men of high ability, but the increasingly complex problems now confronting the states require state lawmakers more able than many who have been elected. Legislators should be persons who are qualified by temperament, experience, and education to represent effectively all segments among their constituents. Above all, they should be persons who, in reaching decisions, will place the general interest above the aims and aspirations of any special interest.

chapter 3
STATE EXECUTIVES
AND JUDGES

The organization and functioning of state governments have been influenced by a variety of factors, including the precedent of the national government, historical events, efforts of political reformers, and regional customs and traditions. It is apparent that the form of the national government has had a pervading impact on the government of the states. Like the national government, all states have separate executive and judicial branches that have coordinate powers with the legislature. But due to other influences the organization and operation of the executive and judicial branches vary greatly from one state to another. Moreover, these two branches differ more from the pattern of their counterparts on the national level than state legislatures, in general, differ from Congress.

STATE EXECUTIVES

The state executive branch has the responsibility for carrying into effect public policy as enacted into law and for performing other functions established by the state constitution. In most states the executive power is not concentrated in the chief executive to the same degree as in the national government, where only the President and Vice-President are elected and all other executive officials are appointed by the President. Instead, in the states the voters customarily choose in addition to the governor and lieutenant governor a variety of other officials, including the attorney general, secretary of state, treasurer, auditor or controller, and superintendent of public instruction. (Figure 3-1 shows the major organizational components of the executive branch of the California state government.) Hence, most states have several elective executives, each of whom is empowered by the state constitution and statutes to perform certain state functions. These officials are not responsible to the governor but are independent of him in the performance of their duties.

The Governor

Historically, the office of governor endowed its incumbent with few important powers. During colonial days the governor, as representative of the English king, was not held in high esteem. Following the Revolutionary War the early Americans continued their distrust of executives, and the states adopted constitutions that provided short terms and relatively little authority for their governors. Gradually, gubernatorial powers and terms of office were expanded. Today the governor is the most visible, important, and influential of the state officials. As in the case of the expansion of presidential power, much of this increase in the stature and authority of the governor has occurred since 1900.

Qualifications and Compensation. State constitutions usually set forth the legal qualifications for the gubernatorial office. Typically, the governor must be a citizen of the United States, a qualified voter, of a certain age —usually 25 or 30—and a resident of the state for a period of time—most often five years. Actually these formal qualifications are of less importance than the political requirements for candidacy, for it is unlikely that anyone who lacked them would be considered a serious candidate even if they were not specified.

Salaries paid most governors are inadequate. They range from $10,000 in Arkansas to $85,000 in New York.[1] In only twenty states are the governors paid $30,000 or more. In addition to the salary, however, most governors receive other perquisites, including the use of an executive mansion as his official residence, a limousine with a chauffeur, and funds for travel, entertainment, and staff assistance.

Election and Term of Office. In all states the governor is elected on a partisan ballot. In a few states candidates for the office are selected in a state convention, but in most states nominations are made in a direct primary. In the southern states where the primary may be more important than the general election, provision is usually made for a "runoff" primary

[1] Interestingly, in 1966 the governors elected in these two states were brothers, Winthrop and Nelson Rockefeller.

between the two highest candidates if no candidate receives a majority vote in the first primary. The cost of a gubernatorial campaign may range from only a few thousand dollars in states in which a candidate encounters only token opposition to as much as $5 million—the amount reportedly spent in 1966 to elect Nelson Rockefeller in New York.

Originally a number of states elected their governors for one-year terms, but since 1920 all governors have been elected for terms of two years or more. At the present time thirty-six states have four-year terms and the others two-year terms. Fifteen states, most of which are in the South, prohibit their governors from succeeding themselves, and in seven others the governors are limited to two consecutive terms.[2]

The Governor's Staff. The size and organization of the governor's staff vary greatly from one state to another. In a number of states the staff consists primarily of an executive secretary and a number of stenographers and clerks. In the more populous states one may expect to find on the staff as many as ten to fifteen secretaries, administrative assistants, and special assistants.

These staff assistants aid the governor by performing a variety of tasks. Some have general responsibilities such as investigating or making studies of special problems, coordinating programs, or writing speeches, but others are given specialized assignments. Usually one staff assistant will serve as a kind of chief of staff, supervising the general operations of the governor's office and possibly making assignments to other staff secretaries and administrative assistants. Typically, other staff aides will include an administration secretary who will maintain liaison with state agencies; a communications or press secretary, whose chief responsibility is keeping the public informed on governmental matters by preparing press releases and arranging radio and television broadcasts and press conferences; a legislative assistant, who coordinates the governor's legislative program and maintains liaison with the legislature; an appointments secretary, who maintains a record of positions to be filled and makes recommendations to the governor on such appointments; and perhaps a clemency secretary, whose responsibilities include advising the governor on executive clemency and extradition processes. In addition, some governors have had a special assistant for research, whose duties include gathering data for the governor's public addresses and for other purposes; and a travel secretary, who advises him on what invitations to accept, arranges his travel and speaking schedule, and may accompany him on trips.

[2] In 1966 Governor George Wallace of Alabama, prohibited by the state constitution from succeeding himself, was able to secure the election of his wife as governor, thus, in effect, circumventing the intent of the law and permitting himself to serve the second term.

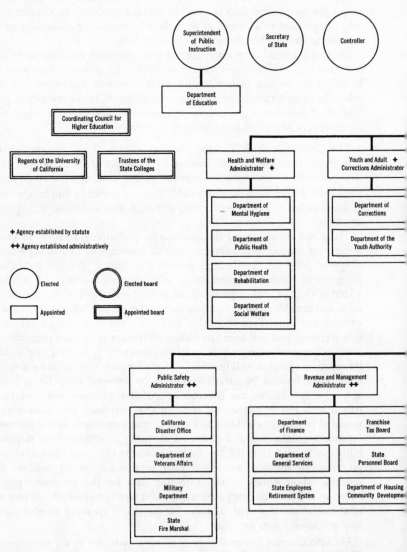

FIGURE 3–1. Major Organizational Components of the Executive Branch of the California State Government.

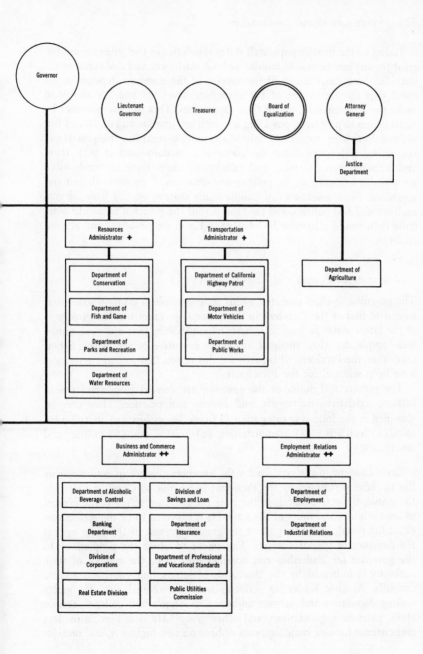

Today, in the heavily populated states the duties of the governor are too great for any one person to handle without intelligent and dedicated assistants. In these states much of the success of the governor depends in no small part on the caliber of his immediate assistants and his ability to make the most effective use of their capabilities. They aid the governor by alerting him to problems, providing him with information and ideas, and furnishing him with recommendations and advice regarding proposed and established policies. Because the governor is in daily contact with them and relies on their judgment and recommendations, these assistants often are a major influence on his policies and decisions. If properly chosen and organized, these assistants can handle many matters on the basis of generally established policies, and thus can permit the governor to devote more time than would otherwise be possible to his major problems and responsibilities.

Gubernatorial Powers and Responsibilities

The governor, as chief executive of his state, occupies a position somewhat similar to that of the President in the national government. The governors of the larger states in particular have responsibilities that are more varied and complicated than those of any other executive officer in the nation other than the President. It is partly for this reason that so many governors have been selected for the Presidency.

The powers and duties of the governor are derived from state constitutions, legislative enactments, and custom and practice. They may be classified in the following categories: (1) civic leadership, (2) party leadership, (3) legislative, (4) administrative, (5) judicial, and (6) military and emergency.

Civic Leadership. As civic leader the governor engages in activities similar to those performed by the President in his role as Chief of State. As the principal elective official of the state the governor serves as the symbol of the authority and unity of the state. He is expected to be the spokesman of all the people and to represent the general interest of the state against the demands of special interests. The extent to which the people look to the governor for leadership and consider him to be the symbol of state authority is indicated by the thousands of letters that governors receive annually. As civic leader he performs many ceremonial acts. He greets visiting dignitaries and delivers addresses to schools and colleges, service clubs, patriotic organizations, and other groups. He dedicates dams, lays cornerstones for new buildings, cuts ribbons on new highways, and presides at the opening of state fairs and public parks. Although these ceremonial activities consume time needed for other gubernatorial responsibilities, the governor performs them, for the public considers them part of his job, and in their performance he enhances his status as the state's chief executive.

Party Leadership. Regardless of the governor's previous role in his party, once he takes office he becomes its titular head in the state. As party leader he is expected to participate in partisan campaigns, to address party rallies, to help raise campaign funds, and to assist his party in other ways. In many states it is customary for the governor to head his party's delegation to the quadrennial national conventions, perhaps as a favorite son candidate. Like the President, the governor's position as party leader may force him to play two roles simultaneously. As civic leader and the representative of all of the people, he is expected to adopt a nonpartisan role. On the other hand, as leader of his party he is expected to work for its success. In brief, most governors are expected to be both a partisan and nonpartisan leader.

The Governor as Chief Legislator. A major responsibility of most present-day governors is to provide leadership in the formulation and enactment of legislative policy. In this respect there has been a close parallel between the growth of gubernatorial and presidential responsibilities, and for similar reasons. During the twentieth century, the chief executive as spokesman for all of the people has become the chief policy formulator. To a large extent the reputation of a governor is determined by his legislative program and his ability to secure its enactment. But as there are strong and weak Presidents, there are also strong and weak governors, and some have not been markedly successful as chief legislators. Most of the governors who have later become President or presidential contenders—such as Woodrow Wilson, Franklin Roosevelt, Thomas Dewey, and George Romney—have won acclaim as outstanding governors largely because of their legislative programs.

SPECIAL SESSIONS. From the standpoint of legislative leadership, governors generally possess powers similar to those of the President. State constitutions usually provide that the governor may convene the legislature in special session, and the constitutions often stipulate that during special sessions the legislature may act only on the subject or subjects specified by the governor in the proclamation calling the session. As state legislatures usually meet less often and for shorter periods than does Congress, the power of the governor to call special sessions is relatively of greater significance than that of the President.

LEGISLATIVE MESSAGES. State constitutions typically enjoin the governor to deliver a message to the legislature on the condition of the state's affairs and to recommend such measures as he shall deem desirable. In this opening "state of the state" message to the legislature, which is usually delivered in person (and in some states may be heard on television and radio), the governor ordinarily outlines his legislative program. During the session he delivers other messages elaborating on these recommendations or adding to them. The authority to recommend proposals implies the power to have bills drafted and to submit them to influential legislators to be introduced. In some states, bills introduced at the request of the governor are referred to as "administration bills" and are labeled with the notation "By request of the Governor."

THE EXECUTIVE BUDGET. During the twentieth century virtually every state has adopted the executive budget, which places with the governor the responsibility for planning the state's expenditures and for recommending measures to provide the necessary funds. In carrying out this responsibility the governor takes the lead in proposing the major appropriations and revenue measures. Of course, the legislature may amend the governor's proposals, but in many states the expenditure and taxation measures approved by the legislature closely approximate those recommended by the governor.

THE VETO. As we have noted in the preceding chapter, in every state except North Carolina the governor participates directly in the legislative process through his power to approve or veto legislation. Moreover, in all but eight states the governor has an important veto power not available to the President of the United States—the item veto, through which he may delete specific proposed expenditures in an appropriation bill. One state, Washington, authorizes the item veto for all measures, not just for appropriation bills. In four states—Massachusetts, Tennessee, Pennsylvania, and California—the item veto permits the governor to reduce amounts approved by the legislature, in addition to eliminating specific appropriations. Thus, in these four states the item veto provides the governor an effective instrument for either eliminating "riders" from general bills or reducing excessive allocations.

In every state the legislature may override a veto. The required vote ranges from a simple majority in some states to two-thirds of the elected membership in others. The time granted the governor for acting on a bill varies from as few as two days (in South Carolina) while the legislature is in session to as many as thirty days if the legislature has adjourned. In a number of states the governor may pocket veto bills, but in others any bill not signed by him becomes a law unless directly vetoed. Some states, including California and New Jersey, have provided that after a specified time following the adjournment of a session the legislature is to reconvene to reconsider all vetoed bills. But in most states bills vetoed after the legislature adjourns must be reintroduced in the next session in order to become law.

EXTRACONSTITUTIONAL POWERS. Like the President, the governor also finds that there are a number of extraconstitutional powers which he may utilize in working with the legislators. To a large degree his success in securing the adoption of his legislative program will depend on utilization of these powers.

If both houses of the legislature are controlled by the governor's party, he may make effective use of his position as party leader to gain support for his policies. Some governors have met regularly with party leaders in the legislature to plan the strategy for securing the enactment of the administration's program. In party caucuses and on other occasions legislators of the governor's party may be urged to vote for the administration's program in order to enhance the position of the party in the state.

One of the governor's primary sources of power is his ability to direct public opinion. As chief executive of the state, his pronouncements and actions are widely publicized. The governor can direct attention to his legislative program in his press conferences, in news releases, in addresses, and in other public statements. Some governors hold weekly press conferences, and others make periodic reports to the people via radio or television. A governor who has a popular program and who is able to communicate effectively with the people may bring pressure to bear on the legislators by appealing directly to the voters.

Governors use a variety of other methods and techniques to persuade the state lawmakers to support their policies. Not uncommonly, governors invite legislators to breakfast or luncheon meetings to discuss legislative measures and may entertain legislators and their wives at dinners. Many governors can still use their power of appointment to gain legislative support. Also, as explained above, many governors assign a staff assistant the task of coordinating the administration's legislative program and serving as a liaison with the legislature; in these states, while administration bills are under consideration members of the governor's staff may lobby the legislators in much the same fashion as the paid lobbyists.

Administrative Responsibilities. State constitutions commonly vest the governor with the "supreme executive power" and enjoin him to "take care that the laws be faithfully executed and that the affairs of the state be efficiently and economically administered." Thus at first glance the governor's administrative powers may seem to resemble those of the President; but in fact, they differ widely. First, the President as the single nationally elected official (with the Vice-President) is alone responsible for the functioning of the executive branch of the national government, but in the great majority of states the governor is only one of several executive officials elected directly by the voters. (See Table 3–1.) The other elected officials are not accountable to the governor for the performance of their duties and may feel under little compulsion to cooperate with him. Second, whereas the President is clearly granted authority over the executive branch on the national level, few state constitutions assign the governor such a clear-cut grant of authority. Third, in a number of states important functions are administered by agencies headed by lay boards, whose members are often appointed or elected for staggered and sometimes long terms. Many of these boards function with considerable freedom from executive control.

One may illustrate the extent to which the governor shares his authority with other officials by briefly looking at the area of law enforcement. Governors generally are charged by their state constitutions with the duty of seeing that the laws are properly executed and enforced. However, the attorney general, who is elected in all except six states, also has law enforcement as one of his principal responsibilities, and much of the law enforcement is done by elective sheriffs and district attorneys and by the city police, who are under the direct supervision of elective municipal officials. Some state constitutions grant the governor the authority, under strict controls, to suspend or remove local law enforcement officials, but obviously such action would be taken only in extreme cases.

APPOINTMENT AND REMOVAL POWERS. Although most constitutions provide for the election of certain executive officers, and in a number of states the great majority of public employees are selected under the civil service system, most governors have extensive appointment powers. In addition to appointing personnel to administrative departments and agencies, governors often are empowered to fill vacancies occurring in other state elective offices, in certain county offices, and in the state and local courts.

The constitutional and statutory provisions authorizing the governor to make appointments differ considerably from one state to another. Usually a governor may make some appointments without the approval of the state senate, and the appointees serve at his pleasure. In other instances appointments may be made only with senate approval, but the appointees may be dismissed at any time. In still other instances appointments must be approved by the senate, and the individuals appointed may be removed only if charges are made and hearings are held, or with the consent of the senate. In states in which senate approval is required for appointments, only rarely is a proposed appointee rejected.

FINANCIAL CONTROLS. The executive budget provides the governor one of his most effective means for controlling and coordinating the adminis-

TABLE 3-1. State Elective Executive Officials

State	Elective Executive Officials	State	Elective Executive Officials
Alabama	8	Montana	7
Alaska	2	Nebraska	6
Arizona	7	Nevada	8
Arkansas	7	New Hampshire	6
California	7	New Jersey	1
Colorado	5	New Mexico	7
Connecticut	6	New York	4
Delaware	6	North Carolina	10
Florida	7	North Dakota	11
Georgia	9	Ohio	6
Hawaii	2	Oklahoma	11
Idaho	8	Oregon	6
Illinois	7	Pennsylvania	5
Indiana	7	Rhode Island	5
Iowa	7	South Carolina	9
Kansas	9	South Dakota	8
Kentucky	8	Tennessee	1
Louisiana	11	Texas	7
Maine	1	Utah	5
Maryland	3	Vermont	6
Massachusetts	6	Virginia	3
Michigan	4	Washington	9
Minnesota	6	West Virginia	6
Mississippi	10	Wisconsin	6
Missouri	6	Wyoming	5

NOTE: In addition to these officials, who are elected by a statewide vote, in some states there are elective boards or commissions, and other state officials are elected by districts or by the state legislatures.

SOURCE: "Elective Offices of State and Local Governments," *Census of Governments,* 1967, Washington, D.C.: U.S. Department of Commerce, Bureau of the Census, 1967.

trative agencies. In preparing the budget the governor, assisted by the finance director, passes upon the plans and programs of state departments and agencies and controls their expenditures. Because the other executive and administrative officials must secure the governor's approval for their proposed expenditures, they are under some compulsion to follow his leadership and to cooperate with his over-all program. Thus the budget submitted to the legislature by the governor contains his recommendations regarding the financial and work programs of each department and agency for the forthcoming year. After the legislature approves the budget, the finance agency oversees the expenditures of the appropriations by the departments and agencies.

RELATIONS WITH OTHER STATES AND THE NATIONAL GOVERNMENT. Among the governor's numerous executive and administrative powers and duties is his responsibility for representing the state in its relations with other states and the national government. On various occasions the governor meets with the chief executives of neighboring states, and most governors attend the Governors' Conference, which meets annually to enable the chief executives of the states to consider problems of general concern. To help solve problems involving his state and the national government, the governor may testify before congressional committees or meet with the President.

The governor's responsibilities in interstate relations is illustrated by the part he plays in the extradition of fugitives from justice. Typically, before a person may be extradited from a state its governor must sign the extradition papers and request the attorney general and the district attorney of the county in which the fugitive is located to assist in the extradition. In order to secure the return of a person who has fled from a state, the governor of that state must request the chief executive of the state to which the fugitive has fled to extradite him.

JUDICIAL POWERS. Like the President, most governors perform certain duties of a judicial or quasi-judicial nature. In some states the governor is authorized to make appointments to the judiciary. In addition, one of the oldest powers of the governor is to grant reprieves, commutations, and pardons to persons who have been convicted of crime. The governor's pardoning power, of course, does not apply to federal offenses. In only a few states can the governor act alone in granting pardons as can the President. Instead, the governor of most states can act only in conjunction with some type of a pardon board. In some of these states the board must agree before the governor may grant a pardon, and in eight states the power to grant pardons is placed in a board of which the governor is a member. Acting on requests for executive clemency consumes much time, and as has been noted above, in some states the governors have assigned one of their administrative assistants the duty of investigating and reporting to him on such applications.

EMERGENCY AND MILITARY POWERS. The governor is the commander in chief of the state militia; hence, he is the military as well as the civil head of the state. The state militia, which has been integrated with the National Guard, is under the jurisdiction of both the state and national government, and is supported largely by federal funds. The phraseology of state constitutions typically authorizes the governor "to call forth the militia to execute the laws of the state, to suppress insurrections, and repel invasions." Obviously, it is not used for either of the latter purposes and only rarely is it called out "to execute the laws of the state." The National Guard in the past has been used to maintain order during prison riots, industrial strikes, or street demonstrations, but in recent years governors have generally preferred to rely on the regular police forces for such purposes. Hence, the National Guard has been called out primarily during times of disasters caused by hurricanes or floods, and occasionally during demonstrations in cities or on university campuses.

In some states the governor's emergency powers have been augmented due to the possibility of a nuclear attack. Legislation has been enacted granting the governor additional emergency powers and authorizing the establishment of civil-defense agencies charged with the responsibility for planning and coordinating civil-defense activities for the entire state. Armed with these additional powers the modern governor has the authority to mobilize the state's agencies and resources to combat any catastrophe.

Other Elective Officials

Early in the history of the United States a large proportion of the administrative activities of the states were performed by elected executive officials and their subordinates. In recent years, as other activities have been undertaken by the states, new agencies have been established and provisions have usually been made for their heads to be appointed by the governor. Today there is little distinction between the kinds of tasks performed by elective officials and the kinds performed by administrative officials appointed by the governor. For this reason, and because of the recognized desirability of coordinating the activities of the various executive agencies under unified leadership, many have urged a reduction in the number of separately elective state executive officials. States with newer constitutions—in particular, Alaska, Hawaii, and New Jersey—elect only one or two state executives, a pattern that is expected to be followed in the future by other states.

Of the various other state officials chosen by popular election those most commonly found are lieutenant governor, attorney general, secretary of state, treasurer, auditor or comptroller, and superintendent of public instruction. The principal duties of these officials will be briefly described.

Lieutenant Governor. In thirty-nine states the voters elect a lieutenant governor to serve as a reserve chief executive. If the governor dies, becomes permanently incapacitated, resigns, or is impeached and convicted, the lieutenant governor becomes governor or acting governor. If the governor is temporarily absent from the state or becomes too ill to continue in office, the lieutenant governor usually may exercise the functions of the office until the governor resumes his duties. As acting governor the lieutenant governor may sign or veto bills, make appointments to vacancies, and exercise other gubernatorial powers. Like the federal Constitution prior to the adoption of the Twenty-fifth Amendment, most state constitutions are ambiguous regarding the conditions under which the standby executive may assume the powers of the chief executive. Stimulated by the discussions of presidential succession, a number of states have recently adopted measures that make more explicit the procedures for determining gubernatorial succession.

In theory, the lieutenant governor is the second ranking officer in the state, but in practice his powers and duties are such that he has relatively little influence or prestige. The principal active responsibility of the lieutenant governor is to preside over the senate, a task that occupies only a few months of his time every one or two years. In some states he also serves as a member of certain boards and commissions. Since the thirty-nine states with lieutenant governors appear to operate no more effectively than the eleven without the office, there is apparently little reason for not abandoning the position.

Those who advocate the retention of the position of lieutenant governor argue that in addition to providing a standby chief executive, the office serves as a useful apprenticeship for persons seeking higher political office. Studies reveal, however, that few lieutenant governors move on to higher political positions other than those who become governor through the death or resignation of the incumbent.

Other political reformers urge that if the office is retained, the governor and lieutenant governor be nominated and elected on a joint ticket, as are the President and Vice-President. Under the generally prevailing practice of separate elections it is possible for the two officials to be from different factions of a party or even from different parties. In recent years several states—including New York, Connecticut, and Michigan—have provided for the two officials to be nominated and elected as a team.

The Attorney General. The attorney general is generally considered the second most important elected executive official in the state. No official other than the governor is elected in more states: the voters elect the attorney general in all but ten states. His responsibilities may be grouped into three categories: First, along with the governor, he is responsible for seeing that state laws are enforced. His actions as the "chief law officer" often set the tone for law enforcement in the entire state. In some states he is authorized to supervise the work of district attorneys, sheriffs, and other law enforcement officers. Second, he represents the state in litigation in which the state is a party to a suit. Third, the attorney general serves as legal adviser to the governor, other administrative agencies, the state legislature, and local government officials regarding their official powers and duties and the interpretation of state laws. Although there is a lack of agreement concerning the best method for selecting the attorney general, most political scientists urge that the pattern of the national government be followed, and the governor, like the President, be permitted to select his own attorney general.

The Secretary of State. The secretary of state, who is elected by the voters in the great majority of states, has a variety of tasks. Customarily, he is the chief custodian of state documents, including all acts passed by the legislature, reports of legislative committees and administrative agencies, and all other official papers, and of the state seal, which he uses to authenticate gubernatorial appointments, proclamations, and other state documents. In some states he registers trademarks and issues certificates of incorporation; before a corporation may conduct business in the state, its articles of incorporation must be approved and filed in his office. Responsibility for the general supervision of elections is often placed with the secretary of state: he certifies the official election results and performs other tasks related to state elections.

The Treasurer. The duties of the treasurer, like those of the secretary of state, are not of a policy-making nature, and there appears to be little reason for electing either official. Yet he, like the secretary of state, is elected in approximately four-fifths of the states. The treasurer is the official custodian of state funds and securities, and in a number of states he also has tax collecting duties. The treasurer's primary responsibility is to provide a banking service by receiving all state funds, keeping them safely, and paying them out on vouchers or warrants. The revenues received by him are deposited in banks, from which payments are made. Surplus funds are usually invested by the treasurer in government securities or deposited in bank accounts that will draw interest. Customarily, the treasurer is also responsible for the sale, redemption, and payment of interest on state bonds.

The Auditor. States vary greatly in their patterns of electing officials charged with fiscal control and audit responsibilities. A number of states elect officials (usually referred to as auditors but sometimes as comptrollers) who conduct both a pre-audit (a check on expenditures as to their legality and the availability of funds before the expenditures are made) and a post-audit (an examination of the fiscal records of agencies spending state money after the expenditures are made). In more than twenty states an auditor is elected who has only post-auditing responsibilities, and in approximately half a dozen states auditors or comptrollers are elected who perform only pre-auditing functions. Most students of state government believe that ideally the legislature should select an auditor who would conduct the post-audit, and the governor should appoint a comptroller or a director of finance who would perform the pre-audit in addition to accounting and other controlling functions.

Superintendent of Public Instruction. In every state there is a department of education or some similar agency, and in more than thirty of them the head of the department is popularly elected, often on a nonpartisan ballot. In the remaining states he is chosen by the governor or by a board. In most states the superintendent of public instruction is an ex officio member of the state board of education or its executive officer or secretary. As the chief state school official, he is generally responsible for the administration and enforcement of state school laws. There is disagreement concerning the best method for choosing the state superintendent, but most political scientists and educators agree that he should not be elected. Educators prefer that this official be appointed by a board selected by the governor, whereas political scientists generally urge that all department heads, including the state superintendent of public instruction, be appointed directly by the governor.

THE STATE JUDICIARY

The legislature and the executive, working together, make the law, often on the basis of the governor's recommendations. Under the separation-of-powers principle the judiciary—the third branch—has the responsibility for interpreting and applying the law. It is true, of course, that the executive departments and agencies also interpret and apply the law. On the state and local levels the attorney general, various state inspectors, highway patrolmen, school officials, sheriffs, and the local police are among the members of the executive branch who often interpret and apply the law. In some instances their actions lead to court cases.

As is commonly known, one of the characteristics of American government is a dual court system in which both the federal government and the individual states have complete court systems. Although the federal courts have concurrent jurisdiction with the state courts in certain kinds of cases and exclusive jurisdiction in others, the great majority of cases in the United States are handled by state and local courts. State courts can handle most of the cases that may be tried in federal courts and many other types of cases in addition; thus the average citizen is more likely to come into contact with state rather than with federal courts.

Organization of State Courts

The organization and jurisdiction of state courts are generally prescribed by state constitutions and statutes. Although the details of state judicial systems vary greatly, fundamentally they are quite similar. In general, there are four levels of state courts: minor courts, of limited jurisdiction; trial courts, of general jurisdiction; intermediate appellate courts; and state supreme courts.

Minor Courts. At the bottom of the state judicial hierarchies are the justice of the peace courts, magistrates' courts, and other courts of limited jurisdiction. Typically, these courts have three principal types of jurisdiction. First, they are authorized to hear and dispose of petty criminal cases, including traffic violations, breaches of the peace, and violations of local ordinances. A large proportion of their cases are of this type. Second, they usually may issue warrants for the arrest of persons charged with major crimes, conduct preliminary examinations into such offenses, and if the evidence is sufficient bind the suspects over for action by a grand jury or prosecutor. Third, they may hear and settle civil cases involving small sums of money (usually $500 or less). In addition, they may perform marriages and notarize documents. In contrast with federal and most other state courts, these are not courts of record; that is, there is no permanent record of their proceedings. If a decision is appealed to the next higher court, the case is heard *de novo*: in other words, a new trial is held, and no reference is made to the previous trial.

Until a few decades ago justice of the peace courts functioned throughout most of the nation; they are still found in most rural areas and in some municipalities. The justice of the peace is typically elected for a two- or four-year period in a township, though he usually has jurisdiction in the entire county. He does not have to be an attorney, and he often has little knowledge of law. Early in the history of the United States, justices of the peace were, commonly, well-respected citizens in their communities; more recently they have seldom been individuals of high prestige or ability, and often they have sought the position in order to supplement low incomes from other occupations. Customarily, they do not receive salaries but are paid from the fees or fines assessed the losing parties in cases— a system of payment that has resulted in a high proportion of convictions in misdemeanor cases and in some instances the solicitation of civil cases.

Because of the general dissatisfaction with the justices of the peace, some states have reduced their powers and others have replaced them entirely. For example, in several states the justices of the peace may issue warrants and subpoenas and perform marriages, but they may no longer try cases. Indiana, Tennessee, and several other states have displaced justices of the peace in the more populous counties; other states, including Missouri, New Jersey, and Colorado, have abolished them throughout the state. These states generally have established magistrates', police, or municipal courts, each with a single judge who is usually an attorney. These judges are typically popularly elected for a limited term and are paid a fixed salary.

In approximately half of the states, courts have been established which have broader jurisdiction than the justices of the peace or magistrates' courts but do not have general original jurisdiction. In some states these are organized on a county basis; in others they are found only in the major cities. Many of the large cities now have unified municipal courts that function under the direction of a chief justice, who has the authority to make specific assignments to the other municipal judges. In some cities these courts are divided into special branches, each of which handles special types of cases such as domestic relations, juvenile, traffic, or small claims.

General Trial Courts. The trial courts of general jurisdiction are usually designated as circuit, district, or superior courts, but other names are used. These are the courts in which most of the important civil and criminal cases originate and are decided. In addition, these courts hear cases on appeal from minor courts. In some states there is a separate general trial court in each county, but more commonly two or more counties are grouped together into judicial districts. In a number of states the larger cities may have their own courts, which are parallel but separate from the other general trial courts of the state. In some of the more populous counties separate courts have been established for civil and criminal cases, and in some instances provision is made for separate probate or surrogate courts, which have jurisdiction over the wills and estates of deceased persons. In less thickly populated areas, however, a single judge will handle all types of cases.

These are one-judge courts, and a jury is commonly guaranteed if requested by a party to a case. Most of their decisions are final, but appeals may be made to higher courts on questions of law. Although relatively few are appealed, a larger proportion of such cases are appealed in the United States than in most other countries.

Intermediate Appellate Courts. In most states, cases may be appealed from the trial courts directly to the state supreme court; however, approximately one-third of the larger states have intermediate appellate courts. These courts—designated as courts of appeals, district courts of appeals, or by a similar title—have as their basic purpose relieving the state supreme court of some of its appellate burden, a function similar to that of the United States Courts of Appeals in the federal judicial system. Some states are divided into districts, with a court of appeals in each district.

These courts of appeals are not "trial" courts in the commonly accepted sense. They are presided over by three or more judges, and they do not use juries. Such courts do not "retry" cases; instead, they review the law and the record of the lower court, and if a retrial appears desirable or more evidence is necessary, they send the case back to the lower courts. In some types of cases a decision of an intermediate appellate court is final, but in other cases appeal may be made to the state supreme court. In some states questions of major importance, such as the constitutionality of a law, may be appealed directly from a trial court to the state supreme court, but in other states all cases must first be appealed to the intermediate appellate court.

State Supreme Courts. In every state, at the top of the judicial hierarchy is a supreme tribunal, called in more than forty states the supreme court and in the remaining states by such names as supreme court of errors, supreme judicial court, or court of appeals. The number of judges on supreme courts varies from three to nine, with about half of the states having seven. In some states, in order to expedite the work of the court, the judges are permitted to sit in two sections, with each section hearing cases separately.

Except for issuing writs, the work of the courts is limited almost entirely to cases appealed from lower courts. Like the United States Supreme Court, one of the functions of the state supreme court is to see that the decisions of the lower courts are uniform. In some states the supreme court, when requested by the governor or legislature, is authorized to give *advisory opinions*, a function not performed by federal courts. Such opinions usually relate to the legality of proposed executive or legislative action. A state supreme court is the final authority on cases concerning the state constitution or laws. Only if an important federal question—involving the United States Constitution or laws—arises may the case be appealed to the United States Supreme Court.

State Judges

Selection of Judges. Most states use a procedure for selecting judges different from that followed by the national government and virtually all other countries. In the national government, and in nearly all other democracies, judges are appointed by the executive and serve "during good behavior" until they die or retire. Prior to the era of "Jacksonian democracy" this system also prevailed at the state level, but in the first half of the nineteenth century the states began accepting the view that in order to ensure responsible government virtually all officials should be elected, and for short periods of time. As new states entered the Union, they provided for the direct election of judges, and some of the older states changed from appointive to elective judiciaries.

Today in approximately three-quarters of the states all judges, or all except those serving on inferior courts, are popularly elected. In four states—two New England and two southern states—the legislatures select the judges. In the remaining nine states—Hawaii, Missouri, and seven eastern states—the judges are appointed by the governor, subject to the approval of the state senate or some other body. Of the states in which judges are elected by the voters, about half use partisan and about half nonpartisan ballots.

Those who support popular election of the judiciary generally endorse the view of Jackson and his followers that frequent election is the best guarantee of responsible government. In addition, they assert that the elective system produces as competent judges as does the appointive system, and that it prevents the governor from exercising undue control over the judiciary. The case against the elective method includes the following points: (1) If judges are elected, party leaders or bosses may determine judicial nominations and elections; (2) the dislike for campaigning may deter highly qualified jurists from seeking judgeships; (3) the electorate may be more influenced by an appealing personality than by legal training and experience; and (4) in rendering decisions elective judges may consider partisan factors and be more concerned with re-election than with the cause of justice. Some of these arguments may not apply in certain states electing judges on nonpartisan ballots. Moreover, because of the central importance of the judiciary in our governmental system, it is unrealistic to assume that political considerations will not play a role in the choice of judges whether they are elected or appointed.

Actually, there may not be as much distinction, as is commonly assumed, between states with appointive and elective systems, in particular if election is by nonpartisan ballot; for, in some states where judges are nominally elected, in reality they are often appointed. In such states the governor is usually authorized to fill vacancies due to death or retirement and to appoint persons to newly created judgeships. Because judgeships are prestigious positions and usually provide satisfactory salaries, most judges wish to continue in office until they die or are able to retire. As incumbents enjoy considerable advantage or may be unopposed in seeking election, once a judge is appointed he is usually re-elected until he dies or retires, at which time the governor appoints another person to the position. Actually, this system has much to commend it. Although the typical voter often finds it difficult to determine which of two or more candidates would make the best judge, from reading newspapers he should be able to decide if a judge has performed well in office. Thus, in practice, judges are often selected by the governor, who is in a better position than the average voter to select judges initially. But periodically each member of the bench must submit himself to the electorate to be judged on the basis of his record.

The American Bar Association for a number of years has advocated a proposal that combines with other advantages the best features of the appointive and elective systems. Variations of their proposal have been adopted by Alaska, California, and Missouri, and in certain metropolitan areas in several other states. Because of the publicity that accompanied its adoption in Missouri, it is commonly referred to as the "Missouri Plan."

In brief, in Missouri a judge of the supreme court, courts of appeals, and certain other courts in metropolitan areas is originally appointed by the governor from a list of three persons, the list having been submitted by a commission composed of both lawyers and laymen. For instance, the commission recommending appointees to the supreme court and courts of appeals consists of the chief justice of the supreme court, three attorneys, and three laymen; the three attorneys are selected by the state bar and the three laymen are chosen by the governor. Alaska and California have similar plans. In Alaska the governor fills vacancies on the supreme court or superior courts from nominations submitted by the judicial council. In California judges of the supreme court and the district courts of appeals are appointed by the governor but are subject to the approval of a commission composed normally of the chief justice, the attorney general, and the presiding judge of the district court of appeals of the district in which the appointment is being made. In each of these states the new judge, after a year or at the end of a term, must submit to a popular election but without opposition. The electorate merely votes on the question, Shall Judge —— be retained in office? Each judge approved by the voters continues in office, and any vacancy created by the defeat of a judge is filled in the same fashion by the governor and the commission or council.

The Tenure and Removal of Judges. An independent and responsible judiciary is generally considered to be dependent upon the method of selecting judges, their tenure in office, and an effective procedure for removing those who are unsatisfactory. The terms vary widely among and within the several states. Typically, the justices on the higher courts have the longest terms. Two states, Massachusetts and Rhode Island, appoint them for life; in New Hampshire they serve until age seventy; after an initial seven-year term in New Jersey, they may be reappointed to age seventy; in the remaining states their terms range from two years in Vermont to twenty-one in Pennsylvania. With but few exceptions terms of lower court judges are shorter than those of the supreme and intermediate appellate courts. Terms of two, four, or six years are most common on lower courts.

Until recently no simple and workable procedure was available for the removal of judges prior to the expiration of their terms. Most states provide for the removal of judges through impeachment or by a joint resolution of the legislature, and nine states provide for the recall of judges. But these methods are rarely used, for they are difficult to invoke and normally are employed only in extreme cases, such as corruption or gross negligence. These remedies are generally considered too drastic in instances when a judge renders poor service because of his work habits, intemperance, laziness, or physical or mental disabilities. In recent years both New Jersey and California have developed procedures for meeting such problems. In New Jersey, if the supreme court believes a judge should be removed, it notifies the governor who appoints a three-man commission to investigate; if recommended by the commission, the governor may retire the judge. California in 1960 established a nine-member Commission on Judicial Qualification composed of five judges, two attorneys, and two lay citizens; this commission is authorized to investigate complaints against any judge and to report its findings to the supreme court, which, if it agrees with the commission, may immediately remove the judge.

chapter 4
LOCAL GOVERNMENT

American local governments, like those in other countries, are the result of a variety of factors, including the prevailing philosophy of government, the historic experience of the people, the geographic environment, and changing social and economic conditions. Since these factors are different in the United States than elsewhere, local government in the United States is different from that in any other country. From Great Britain, the American colonists inherited governmental forms and customs, and the tradition of limited local *self-government*. Among the British institutions transplanted to America are the county and the town, along with the principal local government officials such as the councilman, the constable, and the sheriff.

At the time the American colonies were founded, Great Britain, more than any other European country, had established the custom that local affairs should be managed by local people and not by officials of the central government. Because of the unitary form of government and the great density of population, British local governments now are characterized by more supervision and subordination than are American local governments, but to this day Anglo-American local governments have greater autonomy than those in other major countries. For instance, in France the Ministry of Interior exercises continuous supervision over local affairs and even appoints such government personnel as local police chiefs and schoolteachers. Thus, whereas many Americans consider the system of local control of community affairs to be natural, in most countries a different pattern exists.

69

The local governments of all countries are to some degree under the control and supervision of a higher level of government. In a unitary system such as Great Britain or France, the local governments receive their authority from the central government, usually parliament. In federal systems, such as in the United States or Canada, local governments are under the jurisdiction of states or provinces. In the United States the Constitution reserves to the states the power to create local governments, and the national government exercises no direct control over them. A state legislature, acting within the general limits established by its constitution, may create any number and type of local governing units and grant them whatever authority it wishes.

In the United States the pattern has been for the states to establish one kind of general-purpose unit for rural areas—the county—and another type of general-purpose unit for urban communities—the city, or municipality. Other kinds of local governmental units are the townships, towns, and special districts.

For purposes of enumeration, the U.S. Bureau of the Census has classified local governments into five categories: counties, municipalities, townships, school districts, and other special districts. Each of these units of government has power of a public nature in a given geographic area of the state, has a degree of autonomy, and has the power to raise funds through taxation. In 1968, the Bureau of the Census reported that there were 81,248 local governments in the United States. The number of local governments in the states range from as few as 19 in Hawaii and 61 in Alaska to more than 6,000 in Illinois.[1] Table 4-1 shows that due to consolidation of school districts the total number of local governments has declined.

TABLE 4-1. *Local Governmental Units in the United States*

Type of Government	1967	1952*
Local Governments	81,248	116,756
Counties	3,049	3,052
Municipalities	18,048	16,807
Townships	17,105	17,202
School Districts	21,782	67,355
Special Districts	21,264	12,340

* Adjusted to include units in Alaska and Hawaii which were reported separately prior to adoption of statehood for these areas in 1959.

SOURCE: U.S. Department of Commerce, Bureau of the Census, *Census of Governments: 1967*, Vol. I, *Governmental Organization*, Washington, D.C.: Government Printing Office, 1968, p. 1.

[1] U.S. Department of Commerce, Bureau of the Census, *Statistical Abstract of the United States*, 1968, Washington, D.C.: Government Printing Office, 1968, p. 406.

MUNICIPALITIES

Municipalities may take the form of cities (with which we shall be primarily concerned here) and villages, boroughs, and towns. For the most part, the latter are smaller than cities, have less complex forms of government, and have substantially fewer powers. As will be explained, towns in New England and townships elsewhere differ from municipalities called towns in that they are not incorporated units and perform functions that in most states are the responsibility of counties or villages. Legally, all units of local government are created by the state, but municipalities are customarily ranked above other local self-governmental units because they are general-purpose in character, are formed at their own request, and are incorporated.

Before we describe how cities receive their charters, a brief explanation is needed regarding the relations between the city and state. Although incorporated and autonomous in some respects, cities—like all other units of local government—are legally subordinate to the states. The courts have adopted a principle of municipal law, known as "Dillon's rule," which gives a limited interpretation to municipal powers. In brief, courts hold that cities have no inherent or implied powers and that if there is a disagreement regarding municipal authority, the case is to be resolved in favor of the state.

Municipal Charters

Municipalities are incorporated in accordance with state law. The oldest procedure for establishing a municipality was for the state legislature to enact a special law creating each municipality and establishing its form of government. Under this procedure any alteration in a city's government or in its authority required a subsequent act of the legislature, with the result that the legislature spent much time enacting local legislation. To a considerable extent the special-charter system has been abandoned or modified, but in some states, notably in New England and the South, the special legislation method continues to be used.

To obviate the problems created by special charters, the general charter system, which provides a single charter for all municipalities, was established. But because municipalities range from hamlets to large cities, the general charter system, which requires each municipality to operate under the same charter, proved unsatisfactory, and in no state is this system used today.

The next step was for the state constitutions or the state legislatures to classify cities, usually on the basis of population, and to provide a different charter for each class of city. The classification system was based on the theory that cities of approximately the same size would have similar problems and could therefore operate effectively under the same charter. Although this arrangement was an improvement over the two previous approaches, classification served at times as a subterfuge for special legislation, for through the classification system certain cities could be isolated, and special legislation could thus be made applicable to those cities alone.

A further refinement was achieved with the optional city charter system, now provided by more than half of the states, which makes available several charters. Each municipality may choose the one that it considers best suited for its own particular needs. The number of charters available varies considerably from state to state. Some states provide only two or three city charters, but cities in New Jersey have fourteen charters from which to choose.

Finally, the home rule system was established which permits the local citizenry to draft and amend their municipal charters, subject to the state constitution and laws. Twenty-nine states provide for municipal home rule either through their constitutions or by legislation. In some states it applies to all municipalities, but in others it is available only to those cities over a certain size. The usual practice is for a charter commission to be formed within the municipality for the purpose of designing a charter or amending the existing one. When the commission's task is completed, the charter, or its amendments, is submitted to the voters, who ordinarily must approve it by a majority vote for it to become effective.

The purpose of municipal home rule is to allow maximum flexibility to local communities in determining the structure, procedure, and powers of their government. From this standpoint, home rule provides some advantages over other systems of granting municipal charters. Home rule cities usually have broader powers than do other cities; however, such cities are still subject to state control in any matter of general state concern. Moreover, if charter provisions or local ordinances conflict with general state law, the latter takes precedence. It must be recognized, therefore, that no charter system can provide complete protection against state intervention in local government affairs.

Forms of City Government

In the United States there are essentially three forms of city government: mayor-council, commission, and council-manager. However, within each of these three general types are numerous variations. The mayor-council is the oldest and predominant type: of the cities with 5,000 or more population, more than half have mayor-council governments. Both the commission and the council-manager forms have been developed during this century.

Mayor-Council Systems. The mayor-council form reflects the American preference for the separation of powers, which characterizes the national and state governments. Under the basic mayor-council plan there is an independently elected chief executive, the mayor, and a council, which usually is small—often five or seven members—but may have as many as fifty members. Council members, typically, are elected from wards or districts, but they may be elected at large and even by proportional representation. In small cities council members are often nonsalaried and devote very little time to their positions, but in large cities they may be well paid and spend virtually full time on municipal affairs.

For purposes of analysis, mayor-council cities are usually classified as the weak-mayor or strong-mayor form, depending primarily on the powers of the mayor and his relationship with the city council. In actual practice, most mayor-council cities today do not have either the pure weak-mayor or strong-mayor form but a compromise or blending of the two types.

The weak mayor-council plan prevailed in virtually all American cities during most of the nineteenth century, and variations of it are still widely used, especially in smaller communities. The mayor usually presides over the council and may have a limited veto power. He is considered "weak" primarily because he has little budgetary or administrative power. Under this system there is little central direction or coordination, as both policy making and administration are subdivided among several individuals. The council, in addition to enacting ordinances, typically prepares and approves the budget and appoints several administrative officers, although some are usually elected. Often there are also a number of elective or appointive boards that have policy-making powers. (See Figure 4-1.)

The strong mayor-council form developed toward the end of the nineteenth century and in the early decades of the twentieth century, largely because of the inadequacies of the weak-mayor plan. In the larger cities the weak-mayor systems tend to be replaced primarily because of the need for strong political and administrative leadership. Under the strong-mayor plan, the mayor is granted virtually full authority over the administrative structure of the city government. He is usually the only administrative officer to be elected; the others are appointed and may be removed by

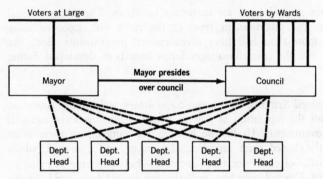

FIGURE 4–1. Weak Mayor-Council Form. (Used by permission of the National Municipal League, New York.)

him. (See Figure 4–2.) The mayor is responsible for the preparation and execution of the budget, for recommending policies to the council, and he has the veto power. The council is assigned a subordinate role in the strong mayor-council system. Its chief responsibilities include approving the budget and establishing municipal policies by enacting ordinances. Council meetings do, of course, serve as a public forum in which councilmen may question or criticize actions of the mayor or other city officials.

The Commission Form. The commission plan of municipal government had its origin in Galveston, Texas, where it was instituted in 1900 after

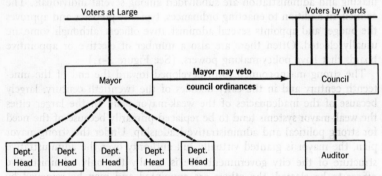

FIGURE 4–2. Strong Mayor-Council Form. (Used by permission of the National Municipal League, New York.)

a hurricane and tidal wave had struck the city. The Galveston commission performed so well and was so widely publicized that in less than two decades more than 500 other cities had adopted this form of municipal government.

The unique feature of the plan is the rejection of the separation of powers principle and the fusion of legislative and executive power in the commission. A small number of commissioners, usually five, are elected at large on a nonpartisan ballot. In some cities a candidate seeks election to a specific position, whereas in others he merely runs for the commission. Each commissioner serves as head of an administrative department; collectively they constitute the city council. Hence the commissioners exercise both executive and legislative powers. There is a mayor, who may be elected separately; or the position may go to the commissioner polling the highest vote. In either event his only power, other than that of a commissioner, is to preside over council meetings and to serve as the formal head of the city. (See Figure 4–3.)

Although initially hailed as a new and highly effective form of municipal government, cities adopting the system soon found that the commission plan has a number of serious defects. Of primary importance is the lack of political leadership, for no single individual provides a focus for rallying community support for public policies. Equally serious is the lack of internal administrative leadership. The division of municipal activities and programs among the commissioners may result in a disintegrated and inefficient government and in higher taxes. Often a commissioner considers his department as his own private domain and resists efforts of other commissioners to coordinate the activities of the various municipal departments. A number of cities have found that a person's ability to win an

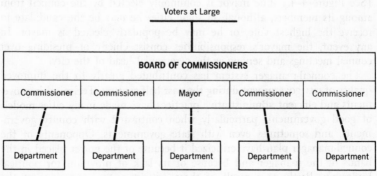

FIGURE 4–3. Commission Form. (Used by permission of the National Municipal League, New York.)

election does not guarantee that he is qualified by training or personality to direct a municipal department. Because of these and other short-comings, nearly half of the more than 500 cities that experimented with the plan have turned to other forms of government, often to the council-manager plan.

Council-Manager Systems. The newest form of municipal government is the council-manager plan, and variants of it known as the council-administrator, chief administrative officer, and mayor-administrator plans. The council-manager plan was first adopted in Staunton, Virginia, in 1908, and it was soon heralded as a major breakthrough in municipal government. By 1967 there were over 2,000 council-manager cities in the United States and Canada, and the number was increasing every year. Approximately half of the cities with 10,000 to 500,000 population have adopted it.

As is the case in the other forms of city government, details of the council-manager form vary considerably from city to city. Typically, an elected council determines policies, makes appropriations, levies taxes, and employs a professional city manager who serves as the city's chief ad-ministrative officer and carries out the council's policies. Most present-day city managers are college graduates who have specialized in public admin-istration and municipal government and have had prior experience in a lesser administrative position in a city-manager system. The manager is not usually given a contract for a definite period of time but has indefinite tenure at the pleasure of the council. The manager appoints and supervises the heads of the city departments, prepares and oversees the execution of the budget, and makes recommendations to the council regarding policies. (See Figure 4-4.) The mayor is commonly elected by the council from among its members, although in some cities he may be the candidate to receive the highest vote, or he may be popularly elected as mayor. In any event, the mayor's responsibilities consist chiefly of presiding over council meetings and serving as the ceremonial head of the city.

The council-manager system has contributed greatly to the improved quality of city government during the past half-century. Technical improve-ments and efficient administrative practices have made many cities models of good government, particularly when contrasted with county govern-ments, and sometimes even with state governments. Opponents of the council-manager plan have criticized it because of the power placed in the hands of the manager and because of its lack of provision for political leadership. Partly as a result of these criticisms, two variations of the council-manager plan have developed.

Some cities that have resisted the council-manager system have instituted

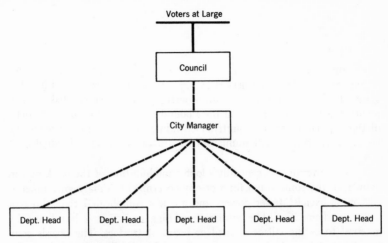

FIGURE 4-4. Council-Manager Form. (Used by permission of the National Municipal League, New York.)

what is known as the council-administrator or chief-administrative-officer (CAO) plan. The essential difference between the council-manager and the council-administrative forms is that the administrator, or CAO, has less authority and prestige than a manager. Instead of being a full-fledged manager, he tends to be a coordinator. The council retains the power to formulate the city budget and to appoint and remove department heads; however, it relies heavily on the advice of the CAO in these and other matters and expects him to supervise and coordinate the programs and activities of the government. The CAO, in comparison with the city manager, must depend more on the power of persuasion than his own authority in performing his tasks.

Although few large cities have the council-manager plan, several have modified their strong mayor-council governments to provide for the appointment of a general manager or CAO. Among the major cities to adopt this modified manager form are New York, Chicago, Philadelphia, San Francisco, and Honolulu. The city governments that provide for a manager as well as a strong mayor have variously been referred to as general-manager, mayor-manager, or mayor-administrator governments. In these cities the mayor continues as the political and administrative head of the government, but he appoints an experienced manager to whom he delegates administrative responsibilities similar to those of the CAO in council-administrator cities.

Villages

There are more than 13,000 incorporated governments in the United States which, because they have less than 2,500 population, are not cities. Together they constitute nearly three-fourths of the incorporated governments, but they contain within their boundaries only about one-twentieth of the population of the country. Depending on the particular region of the country, these small municipalities are called villages, boroughs, or towns.

Village governments generally adopt a modification of the weak mayor-council or the commission form of city government. Village governments, of course, exercise fewer powers and are less complicated than those of larger municipalities. The primary governing agency is a board, usually referred to as the village council or board of trustees. The boards commonly consist of three to nine members who are elected at large or by wards. Customarily the voters or the board elect a chief executive officer, known as mayor or president, who presides over board meetings, directs the affairs of the village, and serves in a ceremonial capacity. The mayor, or president, and board make policy-determining decisions, including those concerning appropriations and taxes, and exercise such ordinance-enacting powers as have been granted the village by the state. The chief executive officer and board members typically devote relatively little time to their village offices and are paid only on a per diem basis, if at all. Other village officers, who often are elected, are a clerk, treasurer, street commissioner, justice of the peace, and marshal. In addition, some villages have an assortment of commissions that are responsible for such matters as public health, streets, water supply, and parks.

The Political Environment and Forms of Municipal Government

There are a variety of reasons why some cities have a particular type of government and others have different systems. In some states the constitution and laws may encourage one form and prohibit others. Apathy and inertia may be the reasons for a city retaining one form of government when another might serve it more effectively. In some instances local interest groups have urged the adoption of a particular governmental system because they anticipate certain advantages from it for their members. Undoubtedly, the general political environment and demographic factors often influence the form of government a city adopts.

Most large cities have mayor-council governments. Only four cities with more than 500,000 prefer a professional manager to the politically elected mayor. The reluctance of major cities to adopt the council-manager form is due primarily to the recognition that, because of the many political and social interests in large complex communities, a political leader is needed who can arbitrate and reconcile the competing demands of interest groups. The reason why so few small cities have managers is obvious: their budgets are insufficient to pay a professionally trained manager.

The amount of partisan activity and the growth rate of cities also tend to be associated with forms of government. Municipalities with manager-council systems are found primarily in states without highly competitive party systems or with a tradition of nonpartisan local elections. The largest number of cities with managers are found in Florida, North Carolina, Texas, and Virginia—southern states where the Democratic party has dominated—and in California—where all local officials are selected in nonpartisan elections. In states with competitive two-party systems there tends to be a concentration of mayor-council cities. For instance, in Indiana, Connecticut, and Ohio—states with competitive party systems—cities in the middle-size range (25,000 to 250,000 population) favor the mayor-council form. This would seem to indicate a relationship between mayor-council systems and environments that demand and reward political skills. There also seems to be a relationship between the rapidity with which a city has grown and its type of government. Cities that have grown very fast often have manager-council systems, possibly because of the need for professional expertise to handle such problems as constructing streets and buildings, providing for water and sewerage systems, and planning for parks and recreational facilities. Mayor-council governments tend to be found in cities with a more stable population, and the commission form is found disproportionately in cities with a declining population. Possibly the political pressures in the latter are better defined and more persistent than in rapidly growing cities.[2]

THE COUNTY

Organized county governments, or their equivalents, exist in all states except Connecticut and Rhode Island.[3] The term *county*, however, does not connote a standardized or uniform governmental unit, but rather a wide variety of geographic and governmental units. The number of counties in

[2] John H. Kessel, "Governmental Structure and Political Environment," *American Political Science Review*, 56 (September, 1962), p. 617.

[3] In Alaska these units of government are designated *boroughs* and in Louisiana *parishes*.

TABLE 4–2. *Size of Counties*

Population-size Group	County Governments	
	Number	Percent
250,000 or more	107	3.5
100,000 to 249,999	169	5.5
50,000 to 99,999	282	9.2
25,000 to 49,999	584	19.2
10,000 to 24,999	1,082	35.5
5,000 to 9,999	550	18.0
Less than 5,000	275	9.0

SOURCE: U.S. Department of Commerce, Bureau of the Census, *Census of Governments: 1967*, Vol. I, *Governmental Organization*, Washington, D.C.: Government Printing Office, 1968, p. 2.

a state ranges from 3 in Hawaii and Delaware to 254 in Texas. Some counties comprise less than 100 square miles; but the largest county in the United States—San Bernardino, California—embraces an area of 20,175 square miles, approximately the size of the states of Delaware, Maryland, and New Jersey combined. In terms of population, counties vary from those with fewer than 500 people to Los Angeles County with over 7 million inhabitants, more people than reside in each of forty-three states. The population density of New York County, New York, in 1960 was 77,195 persons per square mile, whereas in eleven other counties scattered across the nation there were fewer than one person for every two square miles. Obviously, counties constitute highly heterogeneous demographic and geographic units and require widely differing governmental powers and organizations. (See Table 4–2.)

The relationship of counties to their states is not comparable to the relationship of states to the national government. Within the federal system, the states are political entities, which have constitutional status and exercise powers that are reserved to them by the national Constitution, powers that may not be encroached upon by the national government. In contrast, the counties are administrative subdivisions of the states and exercise only those powers granted them by the states. In brief, within the states there is a unitary system of government rather than a federal system.

County Government

As might be expected, considering the variations among the more than 3,000 counties, county governments differ greatly in the services they perform and in their governmental organizations, both from one state to another and within individual states. In New England the county engages in only limited functions and serves primarily as a judicial unit; in the other states with towns or townships those governmental units perform some functions that the counties are responsible for in the remaining states. Thinly populated counties employ only a few officials. However, some urban counties have thousands of employees and perform virtually all of the functions and services usually associated with major municipalities. Thus the states have developed widely differing county organizational structures in response to local needs.

The chief characteristics of county governments are in general a governing board, several other elected officials, and often a complex array of additional officers, boards, and commissions. (Figure 4–5 shows a typical county government structure.)

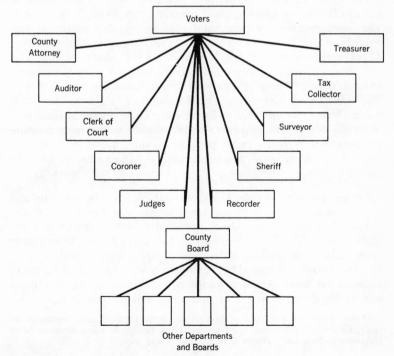

FIGURE 4–5. A Typical County Government Structure.

The County Board. In each of the 48 states with counties, the main county governing agency is a board, named most often the board of commissioners, the board of supervisors, or the county court, but often referred to merely as the "county board."[4] In most instances the board members are elected for terms of two to six years, with four-year terms being the most common. The boards consist of two general types, the commissioner form and the supervisor form.

Under the commissioner form, which is used in approximately two-thirds of the counties, the members of the county board are elected for the specific purpose of serving on that body. Such boards are small, consisting usually of three to seven members, who are often elected by the vote of the county at large but in some states by districts. The board performs executive functions, serves as the county legislature, and occasionally has minor judicial functions. Thus the separation-of-powers principle, which applies to the national and state governments, has not usually been followed in county government. This kind of board, which is almost universal in the southern and western states, is found in other states as well.

The supervisor form consists of a board on which representation is given to the various townships, and sometimes city wards, in the county. The board members are thus first chosen as township trustees or city councilmen, and they serve on the county board in an ex officio capacity. Although the size of such boards depends on the number of townships and cities represented on them, these boards often have 40 to 50 members; and the Wayne County (Detroit), Michigan, board has more than 100. The larger boards customarily set up committees, which consider most matters before they are taken up by the entire board. From the standpoint of serving as a county legislature, the large boards permit more adequate representation, especially in the populous counties. However, as most of the work of county boards is administrative, the smaller boards are to be preferred.

Powers of County Boards. The states establish both the legislative and the administrative powers of the county boards. The legislative authority is limited, consisting primarily of powers of either a financial or a regulatory nature. The county board adopts the county budget, levies county taxes, makes appropriations, and authorizes capital improvements. County boards are usually authorized by the states to enact some kinds of regulatory measures for areas outside municipalities, including zoning regulations and the regulation of places of amusement and the sale of liquor. Ad-

[4] Other names are the board of freeholders, county commissioners, commissioners court, fiscal court, policy jury, court commissioners. George E. Blair, *American Local Government*, New York: Harper & Row, 1964, p. 186.

ministrative responsibilities of county boards include exercising control over public buildings and other property, establishing salaries for certain categories of positions, appointing nonelective officials, and supervising various governmental activities such as the construction and maintenance of county roads. In most states the board serves ex officio as a board of equalization for tax assessments. County boards also customarily conduct elections, supervise welfare, and carry on public assistance programs.

Other Elective Officials. Counties have been created primarily to assist the states in carrying out state programs in local areas. Early in the history of the United States most county officials were appointed. However, during the first half of the nineteenth century the practice (which has continued to this day) of electing most county officials became established. Most students of state government now believe that there are far too many elective officials in most counties, and that a more highly coordinated and efficient governmental system would result if many of the elected officials were appointed by the county board. As it is, each of the elected officials tends to be independent of the county board, which has few if any coordinating powers.

SHERIFF. The principal law-enforcement officer in the county is the sheriff, who is elected in all but three states. In addition to his duties related to the preservation of the peace, he devotes much time to his responsibilities as an agent of the court. He, or a deputy, attends every session of courts of record, and it is his duty to serve warrants for arrest, subpoenas to witnesses, summonses to jurors, and various writs. It is also his responsibility to see that the judgments of the courts are carried out. In criminal cases this may involve keeping persons convicted of crimes in jail for short periods or transporting them to a corrective institution. In civil cases, he may conduct foreclosures on property or seize and sell property to satisfy judgments.

COUNTY OR DISTRICT ATTORNEY. One of the more important of the local officials is the county or district attorney, who is known in some states by other titles, including prosecuting attorney or county solicitor. Customarily, such an official is elected in each county, but in some states he is elected in a district consisting of more than one county. His duties include prosecuting all persons accused of crime; and, if there is no separate county counsel, he advises the county on legal matters and represents it in court.

COUNTY CLERK. The office of county clerk exists in approximately half of the states. Although his duties vary widely from one county to another, they often include serving as the secretary to the county governing board;

performing the duties of auditor or comptroller if the county does not have such an official; serving as registrar of voters and arranging for elections; issuing marriage, fishing, hunting, and other licenses; and serving as clerk of the county and local courts if there is no provision for such an official.

COUNTY TREASURER. An elective county treasurer is found in some or all counties in a majority of the states. His functions consist primarily of receiving and keeping county funds until ordered to pay them out by warrants from authorized disbursement officers. Because the treasurer's records are often largely duplicated by another official—usually the auditor or clerk—some states have either merged the office with some other county office or abolished it entirely.

COUNTY SUPERINTENDENT OF SCHOOLS. Approximately three-fourths of the counties have a superintendent and more than half are chosen by popular election. Due to the consolidation of many smaller school districts in recent years, this office is less important than formerly. County superintendents generally work with the schools outside the municipal areas and advise the local school boards on such matters as school curricula, financial problems, and physical facilities. It is the county superintendent's responsibility to see that the local school districts comply with the state Education Code.

Each of these five officials is elected by the voters in more than half of the counties. Other officials commonly elected include the assessor, the coroner, the surveyor or engineer, the recorder or registrar of deeds, the clerk of court, the tax and license collector, and the auditor or comptroller. In addition, several other officials or boards are customarily appointed. Typically, appointive commissions or boards have the responsibility for such areas as planning, hospitals, welfare, public health, airports, fairs, and libraries.

There is general agreement that the organizational structures of county governments leave much to be desired. The combination of a variety of elective county officials and the use of a number of commissions have created a highly decentralized and uncoordinated governmental system. Because the salaries of elective officials are customarily set by the state legislature and because the general county board is usually required by state law to provide funds for the operating expenses of their offices, the county board has relatively little control over the manner in which these officials conduct their offices. In theory, those who fail to execute their functions effectively will be defeated for re-election by the voters. But because of the long county ballot, the typical voter finds it impossible to inform himself adequately regarding the manner in which each official fulfills the duties of his office.

Optional Charters and Home Rule

A common criticism of county government has been that the states have not permitted the counties sufficient flexibility to adjust their governments to their differing needs and problems. Not uncommonly, a state has prescribed the same governmental structure for its thinly populated rural areas as for urban counties, which perform virtually all functions of a major city. Several states, in order to allow their counties some flexibility in their governmental organizations, have optional charters from which a county may select the one most suited for the particular characteristics of that area. For instance, four such charters are available in Virginia and New York, three in North Dakota, and two in several other states.

Nine states have provided for county home rule. In these states, however, largely due to public apathy regarding county government, relatively few counties have taken advantage of the provisions that permit them to change their governmental structures by drafting and adopting their own charters. The county home rule charters that have been adopted tend to have several similar features. They generally provide for a county board of five to seven members, a chief executive officer (who is usually appointed by the board but who in a few instances is popularly elected), and a reduced number of elective officers.

Modernizing County Government

During the past century the governmental structures of counties in general have changed less than have state or city governments. In most states, in addition to too many elected officials, there are too many counties and too little central direction and coordination of programs and policies. Three-fifths of the states have fifty or more counties, and the number has changed very little. Prior to the automobile, it seemed desirable to have numerous counties in order that the people could travel to their county seat within a reasonable time. Distances have been compressed, but in most states, despite dwindling populations in many rural regions and consequently higher per capita cost of county government in those areas, the local communities strongly resist reducing the number of counties through consolidation.

In addition to the consolidation of counties, another proposal for a reduction in the number of local governments is the merger of cities and counties. In a number of instances where a county is composed almost entirely of a large city—such as San Francisco, Baltimore, or St. Louis—the two have been merged into a city-county.

County Executive Systems. As we have noted, one of the common criticisms of county government has been the lack of administrative leadership and the diffusion of authority among a number of elected and appointed officials and boards. Several counties, recognizing the disadvantages of the "headless" character of their governments and the need for central direction and coordination, have instituted county executives. In a small number of counties there is an elected executive whose duties are similar to that of a "strong" mayor. His duties include appointing most of the nonelective county officials, supervising their activities, and providing advice and information for the county board. Cook County, Chicago, Illinois, has had such an official since 1893. Among the counties that have also created such positions are Nassau and Westchester Counties, New York; and Milwaukee County, Wisconsin.

One of the more noteworthy recent developments in county government has been the appointment, by the county governing boards, of a full-time administrator, ordinarily a person with prior training and experience in public administration. Two general plans, similar to the council-manager and chief-administrative-officer plans of municipal government, have been instituted.

Under the county-manager plan (see Figure 4–6), which is in use in slightly fewer than thirty counties, the governing board makes the decisions regarding public policies by enacting ordinances, approving appropriations, and levying taxes. The manager, who may be removed at any time by the board, appoints his administrative subordinates, directs and supervises the administrative agencies, prepares the budget, and makes recommendations to the board.

The county-administrative-officer plan has been adopted by considerably more counties than has the county-manager plan. In California, where the plan is most widely used, three counties have managers, but thirty-five have county administrators. Under this plan the administrative officer—who may have the title of chief administrative officer, county administrator, or county administrative officer—has less formal power than does a county manager. He does not have the authority to appoint and dismiss other personnel, and instead of preparing the county budget himself, he only assists in its preparation by advising the county board on proposed expenditures. Thus the differences in the powers of a manager and an administrative officer are largely a difference of degree, but the difference has made the latter plan more acceptable to county boards. In actuality, if the administrative officer has a good rapport with the county board and it accepts his recommendations, he has virtually the same power as a county manager.

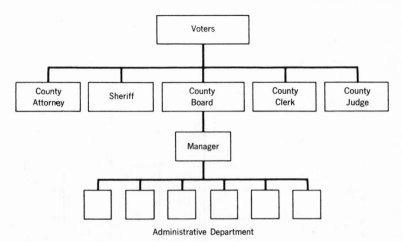

FIGURE 4–6. County-Manager Government.

For either plan to be effective, all or most of the independently elected department heads must be changed to appointive positions; otherwise, the administrative office is largely limited to the powers of persuasion in coordinating the county agencies. The administrative officer plan is especially suited for urban counties with large and highly complex administrative structures. It has been employed successfully in Los Angeles County since 1938. In that county the voters elect the county governing board (Board of Supervisors), the sheriff, district attorney, and assessor. (See Figure 4–7.) The chief administrative officer and the county board make all other appointments. A primary responsibility of the administrative officer is to supervise and coordinate the activities of the more than 56,000 county employees.

TOWNS, TOWNSHIPS, AND SPECIAL DISTRICTS

In addition to municipalities and counties there are towns, townships, and special districts. Problems of nomenclature arise in discussing these units. The word *town* is used in some regions to designate a village, and it often is applied to a particular urban area, as when a person he is going "downtown." Moreover, in some states the terms *town* and *township* are used synonymously. However, as used here *town* applies to the New England towns, and *township* refers to the subdivisions of counties found in fifteen other states.

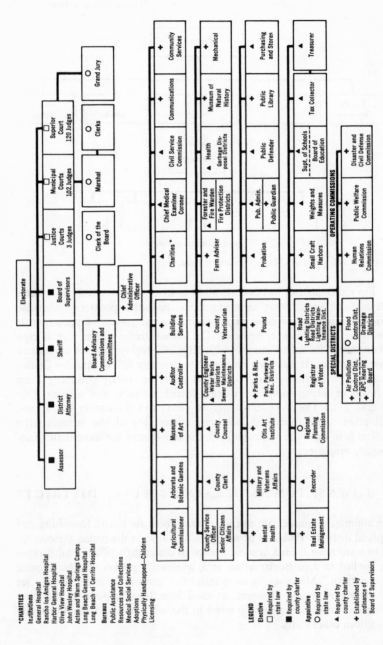

FIGURE 4-7. Organization of Los Angeles County Government.

Towns

The basic administrative subdivisions of states—counties and New England towns—have their origins in early colonial settlements. In the South —largely due to geographic and climatic conditions and friendly Indian tribes—the plantation system developed quite early and the county became the primary unit of local government. In contrast, the early New Englanders—confronted with a rugged terrain, cold winters, and often hostile Indians—usually settled in small communities as religious congregations and farmed the adjacent land.

As the New England town developed, it typically contained one or more communities and the surrounding areas, often with irregularly formed boundaries. Thus in New England since colonial days the town has been the dominant form of local government, and counties have been relatively unimportant. Today virtually all of New England is covered by town governments, except for the areas encompassed by the larger cities, which are usually incorporated. The towns, which are not incorporated, perform most local government functions for the people living within their boundaries. Counties exist in four of the six New England states, but they are of little significance and serve primarily as judicial districts.

The town meeting, which is often cited as the best example of direct democracy since the days of Aristotle and Plato and the Greek city-states, distinguishes the New England town from other forms of local government. All citizens may attend and participate actively in these meetings, which are usually held annually in the spring, but which may be called more often. In these meetings the local citizenry decide on the town budget and taxation measures, reach other decisions regarding public policy, and elect the board of selectmen and possibly other officials.

The board of selectmen, usually consisting of three to five persons, has the responsibility for governmental affairs in the intervals between town meetings. The other town officials—clerk, assessor, tax collector, treasurer, and others—are either elected in town meetings or appointed by the board of selectmen and have duties generally comparable to county officials elsewhere.

The town form of government, with each citizen having the right to participate directly on an equal basis in public affairs, has a strong emotional appeal to many Americans; but in its original form it is practiced today only in the smaller communities. As areas have grown in population and as new burdens have been placed on local officials, some governmental changes have been made. In some of the larger communities the people elect representatives, usually by voting precincts, to represent them at town meetings. Under this system any citizen can still attend town meetings and participate directly in the debates, but only the elected representatives vote. State legislatures have also altered the governmental structure by establishing new offices and boards or commissions with responsibilities for such functions and services as planning, libraries, airports, and parks. A number of communities have employed town managers, who perform tasks similar to those of a city or county manager.

Townships

The township form of government, which now is found in fifteen states,[5] mostly in the Middle Atlantic and Midwestern regions, is patterned after the New England town. New Englanders migrating to other states carried with them the concept of town government, but because of varying circumstances in other areas—especially the enlarged role of the counties and the greater tendency of populous areas to incorporate as municipalities —the township in these states generally assumed different characteristics. In the eastern states—such as New Jersey, New York and Pennsylvania— township boundaries tend to be irregular in shape as are the boundaries of most New England towns. But in the Middle West, government surveyors preceded settled communities, and townships typically are blocked off in squares with sides six miles long. Consequently, in these latter states there are a large number of townships—1,546 in Kansas and 1,822 in Minnesota.

The governmental structure of townships and the functions they perform vary greatly. In about half of the states the township form of government is based on its prototype, the New England town, and provision is made for an annual township meeting in which all qualified voters may participate in the approval of appropriations, in the establishment of tax rates, and possibly in the election of a township governing board. In other states the elected township officials—such as the clerk, assessor, treasurer, and justice of the peace—serve ex officio as the township board.

In an earlier age, when travel was more difficult and life less complex, there were more reasons for township government than today. The general trend is to transfer traditional township functions such as road maintenance, welfare, and law enforcement to cities, counties, or state governments. When such developments have occurred the township may serve no purpose, or possibly only as a district for election administration, tax

[5] Townships are found in Illinois, Indiana, Kansas, Michigan, Minnesota, Missouri, Nebraska, New Jersey, New York, North Dakota, Ohio, Pennsylvania, South Dakota, Washington, and Wisconsin.

assessments, or the election of a representative to serve on the county board. However, it should be noted that as urban townships in some states may provide virtually all the services of cities, people in some urban communities believing that their taxes will be less as a township than as a municipality, have preferred to retain their township status.

There has been a gradual reduction in the number of townships. One state has eliminated its townships altogether, another has transferred all township functions to its county or state government, and others have abolished some townships. There is general agreement among students of local government that townships are not essential. As more than two-thirds of the states do not have this type of local governmental unit, it appears that there would be no major detrimental effect if the existing townships were abolished.

Special Districts

Of the various types of local governmental units, the special districts are the most numerous. These are created under state law for the purpose of providing some limited, and usually single, service. Special districts are customarily classified into two general categories, school districts and other special districts.[6] The most recent census of governments, in 1967, enumerated more than 21,700 school districts and over 21,200 other districts. Since that date there has been a further reduction in school districts, but during the same time there has been an increase in other special districts.

The question naturally arises, Why is there such a growth of limited-purpose districts? Many have been formed to provide a common service for persons living in an area in which there are several cities, counties, and even states. In some instances a city or county may have failed to engage in an activity because only a limited number of people or only the people in one region have desired it. Some special districts have been established as a means of by-passing legal limitations on a city's or county's taxing or borrowing authority.

Special districts are typically governed by a board that may be appointed by the state or a local government, appointed by the several governments served by the district, or, less commonly, elected by the voters. In many instances members of county governing boards or city councils serve ex officio as the governing agency for a special district. Although most special districts possess their own taxing, and often bonding, authority, they generally rely on service charges for the major portion of their funds.

[6] There is a discussion of school districts in Chapter 5 and an additional discussion of nonschool special districts, especially multipurpose districts, in Chapter 6.

There is a perplexing variety of special districts even within a single state. The majority of special districts are found in rural areas in which they are established to provide such services as fire protection, soil conservation, water supply, flood control, mosquito abatement, or road maintenance. However, the larger and more important ones are in metropolitan areas, where they have been created to build and manage rapid-transit systems, airports, hospitals, parks and recreation facilities, public power plants, water systems, and other kinds of facilities. Although the boundaries of some districts are coterminous with those of cities or counties, some such districts overlap city, county, or even state boundaries. In the future, as the proportion of the population living in interstate metropolitan areas continues to grow, the number of special districts that cross state boundaries may be expected to increase.

chapter 5
STATE AND LOCAL FUNCTIONS AND SERVICES

During the past half century the functions and responsibilities of the national government have been greatly enlarged, and much has been said regarding the relative decline of state and local governments. Yet from the standpoints of the number and volume of services performed, the money spent, and the people employed, state and local governments today are more important than ever before; moreover, during the past two decades their activities have grown at a faster rate than have the domestic functions of the national government. In the future, state and local governmental units may be expected to take on additional responsibilities, partly because of the need for an expansion of present services and functions, and partly because of the widely recognized desirability of transferring to the state and local levels the administration of some activities now carried out by federal agencies. (See Figure 5–1.)

Two preliminary observations should be made regarding state and local functions and services. First, there is not a mutually exclusive division of activities and responsibilities between the state and local levels. Instead of a distinct separation, most governmental actions involve groups of officials of each level. State officials cooperate in numerous ways with local agencies, in particular by providing information and technical assistance. Hence the distinction between state and local functions in certain respects is more of an academic convenience than a legal or actual reality. Second, unlike in authoritarian countries, the various public functions and services are performed in an environment of law and order by officials who

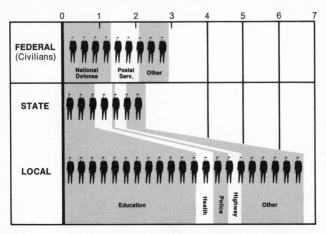

FIGURE 5–1. Government Employees: 1967, in Millions. (*Source:* U.S. Bureau of the Census, *Pocket Data Book, USA 1969*, Washington, D.C.: Government Printing Office, 1969, p. 95.)

themselves are subject to the law. This "freedom under law," which permits each individual to pursue his own interests as long as he does not transgress on the rights of others constitutes the greatest service of all— a service that is difficult to appreciate fully if one has not lived under an authoritarian regime.

EDUCATION

Education is the number-one function of state and local governments. Outside the federal government, teachers and other public-school employees comprise the largest category of persons on the public payrolls, totaling almost half of those paid by state and local funds. On the average, public education accounts for more than a third of local budgets and nearly half of state expenditures.[1] The social consequences of public education overshadow those of all other public programs. Education has been the principal means of social and economic upward mobility in America, and much of the strength and greatness of the nation may be attributed to the public schools.

[1] For example, in 1967 states spent 48.2 percent and local governments spent 39.8 percent of their total general expenditures on education.

The history of public education in the United States may be traced to 1647, when a law was enacted in Massachusetts requiring every town of fifty families to establish an elementary school. Before the Constitution was adopted, Congress provided in the Northwest Ordinance of 1787 that public lands be set aside for the support of schools, and beginning with the statehood of Ohio, Congress made it a condition of admission to the Union that the sixteenth section of every township be set aside for school support. Despite federal assistance, from the early years of our nation, education has been considered primarily a responsibility of the states rather than the national government.

The School District

The independent, single-purpose school district is the basic governing unit for the schools. In four states the schools are administered as a department of county, town, city, or state governments, but in all other states all or most of the schools are operated by independent school districts. In 1932 there were 127,000 separate districts, but through unification and consolidation the school districts have been reduced to approximately one-fifth that number. In twelve states the county is the smallest unit that may constitute a school district; in New England the town or city customarily comprises a district, whereas Delaware has a state-wide school system. But regardless of their boundaries—whether they conform to the state, county, city, town or, as is usually the case, a smaller geographic area— school districts are typically special governmental units.

The governing body of the school district is the school board, which is elected in about four-fifths of the districts and appointed in the others. The board selects the superintendent, approves the appointment of the teachers and other personnel, and establishes the school budget. Operating within the general policies established by state officials, the board determines what courses should be taught and approves extracurricular programs.

State Government and Education

The state legislatures exercise more influence over the schools than is generally realized. Within the legislative chambers the entire education code of law is debated, enacted, and frequently revised. The education code covers such matters as the length of the school year, organization of school districts, powers of local school boards, requirements for teachers' credentials, and in some states even the courses that must be taught. All states have compulsory attendance laws, which usually require persons to go to school between the ages of six and sixteen. An important legislative power is deciding on the formula or policy to be followed in the allocation of state funds among school districts. The legislatures also create state colleges and universities. Because of the importance of these decisions, various groups—including taxpayers' associations, chambers of commerce, labor unions, farm organizations, and teachers' associations—at times appear before legislative committees urging the adoption or defeat of particular policies relating to education.

All fifty states have a department of education or a similar agency, which is headed by a superintendent or commissioner of education, who is elected in thirty states and appointed in the others. The superintendent often shares his authority with a state board of education, which usually is appointed by the governor, but is elected in some states. The board customarily has only broad policy-making powers. The chief education officer and his staff of professional assistants perform a number of functions and services, including prescribing standards for the certification of teachers, administering state school aid, maintaining state standards by inspecting local facilities and curricula, advising on the construction of buildings and the establishment of new programs, and in some states, determining what textbooks may be used.

Various factors have led the state governments to play a more active and direct role than formerly in the public schools. The migration of people from one part of the country to another, from the farm to the city, and from the city to the suburb has accentuated deficiencies in certain school systems. The "knowledge explosion," especially in the biological and physical sciences, has indicated a need for new courses, for revising the curriculum, and for improving the competence of teachers. The philosophy of longer school days and school years, more schooling both in the number of years and in the variety and depth of courses, and the increased birth rate have placed additional economic burdens on the local school districts. Local school officials, forced to rely almost entirely on the property tax for financing the schools, have sought assistance from the state governments, and the states have responded by increasing the amount contributed from state taxes for school support. On the average, state financial aid to local districts has increased from less than one-fifth of the cost of operating the schools in 1930 to more than twice that today, and in four states two-thirds of the school budgets are paid from state funds. See Table 5–1 for recent data on public-school expenditures.

Higher Education

Prior to the passage of the Morrill Act, or the Land Grant College Act, in 1862 there were very few public colleges and universities in the United

TABLE 5-1. *Expenditures of Public Schools: 1968*

State	Total (millions of dollars)	Average per pupil [1]	State	Total (millions of dollars)	Average per pupil [1]
United States	31,511	$623	Missouri	586	$532
			Montana	120	624
Alabama	395	403	Nebraska	198	492
Alaska	83	976	Nevada	87	626
Arizona	252	640	New Hampshire	97	571
Arkansas	228	441	New Jersey	1,207	807
California	4,088	639	New Mexico	200	640
Colorado	362	621	New York	3,494	982
Connecticut	458	715	North Carolina	629	461
Delaware	100	665	North Dakota	98	554
Florida	945	554	Ohio	1,540	591
Georgia	592	508	Oklahoma	347	547
Hawaii	134	659	Oregon	344	664
Idaho	101	517	Pennsylvania	1,793	657
Illinois	1,456	621	Rhode Island	125	721
Indiana	860	612	South Carolina	298	427
Iowa	419	580	South Dakota	105	586
Kansas	326	582	Tennessee	461	461
Kentucky	351	475	Texas	1,415	493
Louisiana	589	618	Utah	195	512
Maine	129	490	Vermont	67	615
Maryland	722	702	Virginia	665	554
Massachusetts	762	728	Washington	561	613
Michigan	1,510	628	West Virginia	219	484
Minnesota	726	725	Wisconsin	706	691
Mississippi	237	346	Wyoming	63	690

[1] In average daily attendance.

SOURCE: U.S. Bureau of the Census, *Pocket Data Book, USA 1969*, Washington, D.C.: Government Printing Office, 1969, p. 159.

States. Now more than two-thirds of college students attend public colleges. The Morrill Act set aside public land in each state, the sale of which was to provide funds for the establishment of a college or university. This act was thus instrumental in the establishment of the state universities, which are now the major institutions of higher learning in most states. Subsequent to the founding of the state universities, a number of states started normal schools or teachers colleges, many of which have later become general state colleges. In recent years several states have established new branches or campuses of their state university as well as new state colleges. Most states also have junior or community colleges that offer two-year programs. The junior colleges, which in terms of numerical growth are the fastest-growing type of institution of higher education, are customarily under the control of a local school board, but are usually heavily supported with state funds. Today, with more than half of the graduating high school students enrolling in college and the proportion increasing virtually every year, considerable attention is being given to developing additional facilities.

HEALTH AND WELFARE

Public Health

State government health programs are usually administered by a state board or by a state health department. Typical functions of state health departments include collecting vital statistics; administering sanitary codes and inspecting drinking water, dairies, restaurants, and packing plants; providing assistance to local health departments and to local communities in the development of hospitals; exercising environmental control with respect to air and water pollution and occupational and radiological hazards; and providing for maternal and child care as well as preventive medical services in the fields of chronic and communicable diseases. States, with the assistance of federal grants, provide large subsidies for medical education; in fact, almost half of the medical schools in the United States have been established and are maintained by the states. States also are responsible for examining and licensing doctors, dentists, and nurses.

The division of responsibility between state and local public health departments depends upon a variety of factors, including whether the state's population is largely urban or rural. In regions where there are no sizable municipalities public health responsibilities may be placed in the hands of a physician who also has a private practice. In these areas most public-health functions are performed by state officials, but in the more populous states most of the public health services are usually performed by municipal or county health departments. In many large cities the head of the health department is usually a professionally trained public health administrator who heads a large and specialized staff of medical doctors, nurses, inspectors, and other employees. Although most of their efforts are directed toward the discovery and control of communicable diseases and other health problems, much attention typically is devoted to preventative measures. States and local communities have increased their hospital building programs with the assistance of federal grants, so that now half of the hospital beds are in state and local government hospitals.

Mental Health

There has been a notable change in public attitudes in recent decades toward the mentally ill and mentally retarded. Formerly, most states limited their activities to providing custodial care in insane asylums: drug addicts and alcoholics were commonly placed in city or county jails, and retarded children were cared for by their parents or were placed by them in privately operated homes or schools.

The state governments now make provision for the treatment of thousands in numerous mental hospitals, neuropsychiatric institutes, clinics, and daytime treatment centers; other thousands are treated in various public and private community facilities. Most states still have not established programs and facilities equal to those of some Western European countries, but the goal is now rehabilitation wherever possible rather than custody. Today nearly twice the proportion of individuals are admitted to mental hospitals as twenty years ago, but due to improvements in methods of treatment and to the development of programs of aftercare, in some states as many as 85 percent of those admitted are discharged within a year, and many after only two or three months.

Social Welfare

Possibly in no other area has there been during recent years a more significant assumption of governmental responsibility than in the field of social welfare. Prior to the Great Depression most of what are now considered welfare services were supplied either through local charities or relief administered by city or county officials. Except for providing workmen's compensation, neither the states nor the federal government had indicated more than a passing interest in welfare. The extent and length of the Depression and the amount of hardship and suffering that accompanied it produced widespread changes of attitude regarding the responsibility of government. Formerly government had granted financial assistance and subsidies to railroads, other businesses, the farmers, and veterans. In the 1930s it became more generally recognized that the poor and the unfortunate also merited public assistance.

The first major federal legislation was the Social Security Act of 1935. Although resisted by certain segments of the population for years, the provisions of this act, with the various liberalizing amendments, are now almost universally accepted and provide the backbone of the federal security system. Under these provisions the federal and state governments have operated a well-established program of unemployment insurance, old-age assistance, disability insurance, and aid to the blind, the totally disabled, and to families with dependent children. In 1964 and 1965 Congress adopted legislation enacting the "anti-Poverty" and "Medicare" programs. In brief, a virtual revolution has occurred within a period of three decades regarding the responsibilities of the various levels of governments for social welfare. Today the federal government supplies much of the impetus and funds, but most of the administration is in the hands of state and local officials.

PUBLIC SAFETY

The protection of persons and property is one of the basic and oldest functions of government. According to the British political philosopher John Locke, government was first established to protect "life, liberty, and property." In the broader sense, virtually all governmental activities are directed toward promoting the public safety. More precisely, however, protecting the public safety means defending the lives and the property of individuals against natural disasters, law violators, and fire.

Although the state governments provide for the inspection of businesses and other enterprises where there is a high fire danger and for fire protection for state forests and public lands, most fire protection is handled by city and county governments. Fire and police protection together constitute the largest expenditure item of local governments.

The United States differs from most other countries by the fact that police protection and law enforcement have traditionally been exercised primarily by local governments. Under the American constitutional system federal officials can take action only against persons accused of violating federal laws or the Constitution. Moreover, the United States has never had a national police force, and many Americans would oppose the creation of one. Federal law-enforcing activities are performed principally by the Federal Bureau of Investigation of the Department of Justice, the Secret Service of the Treasury Department, postal inspectors, narcotics agents, treasury inspectors, and border patrol and immigration officials.

Law-Enforcement Agencies

State Police. Virtually all states now have some type of state police force, although the pattern of organization varies considerably. In some states there is a consolidated highway patrol and state police; in others they are organized separately; and in still others there is only a highway patrol with jurisdiction limited primarily to the highways in unincorporated areas. In addition, the states have other law enforcement officials, including fish and game wardens, liquor enforcement officials, fire marshals, and other specialized forces.

State police organizations have developed in response to a variety of circumstances and needs. The oldest state police organization, the Texas Rangers, established in 1835, was founded to supplement the military forces and to patrol the border. Most state police systems were created during the early decades of this century as a response to the development of the automobile and the general recognition that the county sheriff and the municipal police were unable to combat successfully the growth of organized crime and to maintain highway safety. The establishment of a state police was often opposed by city and county officials and community leaders who resisted the intervention of the state in local affairs. However, as evidence mounted regarding the rising crime rate and the inability of the existing police organizations to cope with the problem, opposition to the formation of a state police generally dissipated. Today there is far more cooperation between the state police and federal law officers and the local police than is commonly realized.

Sheriff. In earlier days protection of the public was largely in the hands of untrained part-time elected officials. The offices of county sheriff and town marshal or constable were transplanted in this country by settlers from England. In all but very small communities the constables have generally been replaced by municipal police, but the sheriff is still the primary police officer in counties. These officers are responsible for the enforcement of state laws as well as the local ordinances adopted by the county governing boards. Customarily, the sheriff and his deputies exercise police jurisdiction only in unincorporated parts of counties and leave the enforcement of laws in the municipalities to the city police.

In every state except Alaska and Rhode Island the sheriff is elected by the voters, customarily for a two- or four-year term. The sheriff's salary is usually quite low, but because he typically receives fees, a mileage allowance, and is paid for boarding prisoners, some sheriffs receive a higher remuneration than do most of the other local or state officials. In some counties the sheriff and his deputies are competent and well trained and have modern equipment. More often the office is filled by a person who has had little interest or training in crime detection and prevention and who has run for the office primarily because of the income opportunities. Students of local government generally recommend that the elective sheriff be eliminated and that his duties be turned over to qualified appointive officials.

Municipal Police. In virtually every city today a police chief heads a department which, depending on the size of the municipality, may range from only a few patrolmen to hundreds of well-trained and highly specialized personnel. In the larger cities the police departments are organized in a semimilitary fashion, with divisions that handle the different aspects of police work: traffic patrol, detective, vice, juvenile, and record-keeping. With police academies and institutes, scientific laboratories, telecommunications, and high-speed vehicles, American municipal police are the best trained and equipped in the world. Nevertheless, our crime rate is higher than Europe's and has increased sharply in the decades since World War II.

Between 1950 and 1960, while the population increased 18 percent, the absolute increase in crime was 98 percent; and between 1958 and 1964 crime increased almost six times faster than the population.[2] Analysis of crime rates shows that not only is crime more prevalent in cities than in rural areas, but that for most regions of the nation, the larger the community the higher the crime rate. For instance, in 1968 Philadelphia reported 2 robberies for every 1,000 inhabitants, Houston 4, Chicago 5, New York 7, and Detroit 9. Although the factors responsible for the high crime rate in the United States are numerous and complicated, one factor is the relatively small number of police in American cities in comparison with European cities. Other factors include the greater mobility of the American people, a more permissive society with fewer community restraints, fewer records maintained on individuals, and the large number of political jurisdictions. The growth of suburban areas in the United States has multiplied the number of independent police departments; within a radius of fifty miles of Chicago, for instance, there are more than 350 communities with their own police departments.

Prosecution of Crime

Each state has an attorney general who, along with the governor, is responsible for the enforcement of state laws. In some states the attorney general is specifically authorized by the constitution to supervise the work of local law-enforcement officials. The actual prosecution of suspected lawbreakers, however, is almost entirely in the hands of the county or district attorney. These officials are usually elected for a two- or four-year term, but in Connecticut they are appointed by the judges, and in Delaware and Rhode Island, by the state attorney generals.

[2] United States Department of Justice, *Uniform Crime Reports,* July 1, 1964, Washington, D.C.: Government Printing Office, 1965.

The National Guard

Since World War I the state militias have been integrated with the National Guard, whose primary purpose is to serve as a trained reserve of combat troops for the active army and air force. The federal role of the National Guard is recognized by the fact that the national government provides 90 percent of the funds which the Guard requires annually. However, until Guard units are called into active service—which is rare except during wartime—the units are under the direction of the governor and are available to help deal with a natural disaster or civil disorder.

The effectiveness of National Guard units varies widely, depending to a large extent on the caliber and ability of the officers, who are appointed by the governor. Partly because of the lack of training and experience of National Guard personnel, governors generally prefer to use state and local police forces to handle civil demonstrations and disorders; however, if disorders reach a magnitude too large to be managed by the regular police forces, the National Guard is usually called out. In recent years several proposals have been submitted by Presidents or Secretaries of Defense for reducing the size of the National Guard and reorganizing it into more effective units. Such proposals have generally been opposed by governors and congressmen who often for political reasons have wished to see the existing units retained.

Civil Defense

During the decades following World War II a number of states enacted legislation providing for civil defense councils or state disaster offices. Officials appointed to these offices were enjoined to develop state civil defense and disaster plans that could be put into effect in case of an enemy attack or a disaster resulting from natural causes. At the federal level, within the Executive Office of the President the Office of Emergency Preparedness was established to work with, and assist, state and local authorities in developing plans for the protection of the population.

TRANSPORTATION, RECREATION, AND NATURAL RESOURCES

Transportation

Many activities of government are largely unnoticed, but not those in the fields of transportation and public works. Annually state and local governments spend literally millions of dollars planning and constructing highways, bridges, public buildings, airports, and other public facilities. Of these various kinds of projects, highways, streets, and public transportation systems require the largest outlays of funds. Indeed, after education, highway construction is the second largest item in state budgets. (See Figure 5–2.)

It is a truism that "America moves on wheels," and it is the task of state and local governments to build the streets and highways for those wheels. Public roads are generally of four types: country roads, city streets, state highways, and federal highways. Formerly, local governments built and maintained virtually all of the roads. Now state governments have the responsibility for the latter two types and some state governments provide assistance on country roads and certain city streets, in particular city expressways or freeways.

Since 1916 the national government has given grants-in-aid to states for building highways. The state plans and constructs the federal highways in accordance with standards established by the national government, which contributes a large share of the cost. The Federal Highway Act (1956) provides for a system of interstate superhighways, 90 percent of the funds for which come from the federal government. When completed in about 1972, there will be more than 40,000 miles of superhighways connecting virtually every city with a population of 50,000 or more.

Transportation is one of the pressing problems in metropolitan areas. Rapidly expanding air traffic has led to congested airports in many cities and the demand that additional air facilities be constructed. Providing expressways, streets, and parking lots consumes enormous sums of money and acres of valuable urban land that are removed from the tax rolls. In the larger metropolitan areas heavy traffic and air pollution—to which automobiles, buses, and trucks are contributors—are political and economic issues of the first magnitude. Means must be found, within the next few years, of providing mass rapid-transit systems that can quickly move thousands of people between the suburbs and central cities. San Francisco, Los Angeles, and Washington, D.C., are currently planning, financing, and constructing rapid-transit systems. Partly because of the wide dispersal of individuals in urban areas, mass transportation systems are difficult to plan and tremendously expensive to construct.

Recreation

With shorter workweeks, higher salaries, pension systems that permit early retirement, and longer life expectancy, individuals have more opportunity than formerly for recreation. In the decades since World War II there has been an upsurge of support for the public development of recreational facilities by all levels of government. The national government has acquired more land for national parks and forests, and has developed new campsites and family outing areas. All states maintain parks and several—especially California, Oregon, New York, Michigan, and Pennsylvania—have excellent state parks and other recreational areas. A number of states in recent years have acquired additional beaches, and mountainous or timber areas for parks. Municipalities have also found strong popular support for expanding their recreational facilities. Many cities have built and maintain parks, play-grounds, swimming pools, youth centers, and facilities for senior citizens. Even with the occasional aid of private philanthropy, municipalities with growing populations have needs for land and other recreational facilities that have far outraced the supply.

Natural Resources

The states as well as the national government have been aware of the need to protect and develop the natural resources. Due in part to our nation's agrarian heritage and the overrepresentation of the farmer in legislative assemblies, agriculture has long received more governmental assistance than most other areas. Every state has a department of agriculture and at least one agricultural college with a related agricultural experiment station where research is conducted in an effort to improve farming methods and farm products. All three levels of government cooperate to aid the farmer through the county farm extension agent, who is paid in part with federal funds and works under the supervision of the state agricultural college.

States engage in a variety of activities aimed at conserving natural resources. Most states own and administer state forests, maintain fire-fighting equipment, and operate nurseries to replace trees that are cut or burned in forest fires. The oil industry is regulated by a network of state and federal laws and interstate agreements that limit and prorate production. Due in part to the efforts of sportsmen, states have laws regulating hunting and fishing and maintain fish hatcheries to restock lakes and streams.

Fresh air and water are natural resources that most people have taken for granted, but smog now blankets many urban areas, and water pollution is a widespread problem. No one knows how much damage is done to people physically and psychologically from living in a polluted atmosphere, but in 1966 in one three-day period of intense air pollution 168 deaths in New York were attributed to smog. Many plants and trees cannot live in a smog-polluted atmosphere. The direct annual economic cost of smog to the nation has been estimated to range from $4 to $11 billion. Many cities and states have attempted to alleviate the problem, but year after year air pollution becomes worse in many metropolitan areas. Backyard trash burning has been prohibited in several cities, but the main causes of air pollution are automobiles, buses, and trucks, and certain types of industries. Realizing that state and local governments cannot cope with the magnitude of the problem, Congress in 1967 enacted the Air Quality Act, which authorizes the Secretary of Health, Education and Welfare to attack the problem on a regional basis where air pollution overlaps state boundaries. In 1969 President Nixon created within the Executive Office of the President the Environmental Quality Council to coordinate efforts on different levels of government to prevent air and water pollution and to protect other natural resources.

REGULATION OF ECONOMIC ACTIVITY

Because of the complexity of life in contemporary industrial America, one of the important functions of state government is to regulate certain aspects of economic life. Although some people complain of excessive regulations, Americans are subjected to less regulation than people in most European countries or in some less highly populated democracies such as Australia and New Zealand. Moreover, it should be noted that the principal purposes of governmental regulations include promoting an orderly social and economic system that will attract new economic enterprises and aid the established ones to prosper, and protecting the rights of the people. Of the various regulatory activities of state and local governments the following are some of the more important.

Corporation Charters and Security Issues

Although some types of corporations have federal charters, most corporations receive their charters from a state. Earlier in the country's history state legislatures often granted charters by special acts; now charters are usually issued in accordance with general corporation laws, and most states prohibit the granting of corporation charters by special act. A corporation chartered in one state may engage in business in another, subject to the laws of that state, which may include special regulations for out-of-state corporations.

The federal Securities and Exchange Commission regulates the major stock and commodity markets, but all states except Nevada also have regulations to protect the public against fraudulent securities. In a number of the states the agency handling corporation applications also reviews the requests to sell corporation stocks and bonds. As in the case of federal regulations, state regulations are not intended to guarantee the buyer a profit, but to prevent frauds and to require full disclosure of information.

Banks, Savings and Loan Associations, and Insurance Companies

There are two parallel commercial banking systems in the United States—national banks chartered and regulated by the federal government, and state banks under state jurisdiction. State control over banks includes bank organization and management, amount of capital stock, liabilities of directors and stockholders, amounts of assets and investments, reserves, inspection of bank records and accounts. Most state banks are members of the Federal Deposit Insurance Corporation, and are thus also subject to federal regulation and inspection. Similar regulations apply to savings and loan institutions and to small-loan companies, which are granted state charters or licenses.

In no other country of the world has the insurance business been developed in a fashion similar to that in the United States. Americans buy and sell insurance against death, sickness, and injuries, unemployment, accident, fire, theft, storm damage, and other "acts of God." Thus insurance has become big business. The United States Supreme Court has ruled that the national government may regulate insurance under its authority over interstate commerce, but as Congress has not acted, the states provide the only regulation. States vary considerably in their regulations, and some do not provide sufficient protection for the insured. States generally have an insurance commissioner, whose duties include licensing insurance companies, exercising surveillance over their financial conditions to determine if they maintain adequate reserves, investigating complaints against companies or agents, and advising and assisting in the collection of taxes on insurance companies.

Public Utilities

Public utilities are those businesses or industries which, because of their monopolistic nature, are subjected to special governmental regulations. It is easier to list types of businesses that are public utilities than to formulate a precise statement defining them. Well-known examples are the water, gas, electric power, telephone, telegraph, bus, and railroad industries. They are distinguished from others by the fact that they provide essential services in areas where competition is not practical, the government grants them a franchise to operate, and the government usually gives them certain rights, such as the power of eminent domain. Government regulation of public utilities was approved by the United States Supreme Court in 1877 in the case of *Munn* v. *Illinois*. Public utilities operating in interstate commerce may be regulated by agencies established by Congress, others may be controlled by the state or local governments where they operate, and some are subject to regulation by both the national and the state governments.

Most states have a public-utility commission, which exercises powers similar to those held by the federal Interstate Commerce Commission and the Federal Communications Commission. The number of commissioners varies from one in Rhode Island to seven in South Carolina, with three the average number. With regard to utilities operating within the state, the commissions usually have authority to grant franchises and permits, to approve the issuance of securities, to set rates and charges, and to ensure efficient performance and continuity of service. In general, these commissions have the responsibility to see that the public utilities operate in the best interest of the public.

Labor Relations

The national government since the 1930s has played a more significant role than the states in the protection and regulation of labor and industrial relations, yet the latter perform a number of important functions. State regulations apply not only to the millions of workers in intrastate industries not covered by federal regulations, but also to certain problems and issues affecting all workers in the state.

Labor Relations and Standards. Since the enactment of the National Labor Relations Act in 1935, the national government has exercised jurisdiction over most phases of labor-management relations in industries that are directly or indirectly involved in interstate commerce. However, purely intrastate businesses are not covered by federal legislation, and Congress has also specifically left to the states control over other labor-management matters. For instance, states may prohibit the "union shop," which is an agreement between a union and an employer requiring workers who are not union members at the time of employment to join the union. During the last two decades more than a third of the states (mostly in the South and West) have enacted so-called "right-to-work" laws, which forbid the union shop.

The more progressive states have long had regulations relating to working conditions and labor-management regulation. In recent decades the national government has enacted legislation in those areas, but the states still have important responsibilities. Laws have been passed relating to health, safety, and comfort conditions in factories, plants, mines, and other places of employment. State officials regularly make inspections to enforce the maintenance of standards regarding such matters as lighting, ventilation, heating, fire escapes, and safety guards around machines.

Most states have minimum-pay and maximum-hours laws for women and young people who work in industries not covered by similar federal legislation. However, only a few states have minimum-pay laws for men; and state maximum-hours laws usually apply only to men working in dangerous occupations or in jobs where public safety is involved, such as the driving of buses or trucks. All states have child-labor laws that regulate or prohibit the labor of children under a certain age, usually fourteen or sixteen. Before the enactment of The Fair Employment Practices Act of 1964 approximately half of the states had laws that prohibit discrimination in employment because of race, color, creed, or national origin.

Unemployment Insurance and Workmen's Compensation. In an industrial society it is highly important for an individual to have regular employment and income. States generally have a department of employment that serves several purposes, including helping workers find jobs and employers find needed employees. States cooperate with the national government in providing a system of unemployment compensation for those out of work. The states collect from employers a tax levied on payrolls which is deposited in that state's account in the United States Treasury Unemployment Insurance Trust Fund. From this fund unemployed workers receive benefits for a limited number of weeks—the time and benefits depending on the particular state's program.

All states have workmen's compensation programs that provide payments to employees injured (or to their beneficiaries if killed) while on the job, but the coverage is confined almost exclusively to manufacturing workers. In most states a board establishes the amount of the award in each case. Employers are required either to take out insurance or furnish evidence of the ability to make such payments if necessary. About one-fourth of the states have created self-supporting, nonprofit agencies to provide industrial accident insurance.

STATE AND LOCAL FINANCE

Expenditures

A comparison of the expenditures of the different levels of government serves as a general indicator of the rate of growth of the national, and state and local governments. Prior to the 1930s state and local budgets collectively exceeded that of the national government. Since then—largely due to the Great Depression, World War II, and the wars in Korea and Vietnam— the federal budget has exceeded that of the states and local governing units by approximately a 60–40 ratio.[3] However, in the period immediately preceding the build-up of American forces in Vietnam the rate of growth of state and local spending surpassed that of the national government. To illustrate, in the decade 1952–1962 federal spending rose 25 percent, whereas state and local expenditures increased 128 percent.[4]

The three functions requiring the largest outlays of state funds are education, highways, and public welfare. (See Figure 5–2.) To a large extent, expenditures of these activities are established by state constitutions and laws and by federal legislation. Consequently, the state legislatures have relatively little discretion in making major adjustments in these expenditures on a year-to-year basis. Much of the money spent by counties and cities is also for education, streets and roads, and public health and welfare, but in many municipalities the largest budget item is for public safety—police and fire protection.

Revenue

One of the major functions and problems of government is raising the funds necessary to pay for its many and varied operations. State and local governments are limited in raising revenue by provisions of the federal Constitution and the constitutions of the states. In brief, among the limitations in the national Constitution are those prohibiting states from taxing exports or imports or interstate commerce; from employing the taxing power to interfere with federal activities; and from using the taxing power to deprive people of their property without due process of law or to deprive them of the equal protection of the law. Although these provisions of the Constitution do not greatly restrict the actions of the states, they do provide the basis for numerous court cases. For instance, cases often arise regarding the right of a state to tax property outside the state purchased or owned by its residents.

State constitutions also contain provisions limiting the taxing power. Customarily, constitutional provisions prohibit the taxing of certain types of property—for instance, property used for charitable, educational, or religious purposes. Many state constitutions specify the kinds of taxes that may be imposed by either the state legislature or local government units, and forbid others.

[3] For example, for the fiscal year 1967, excluding intergovernmental transfers, the federal government had expenditures of $151.8 billion; the states $39.7 billion; and local governments $67 billion. *Congressional Quarterly Weekly Report* (January 17, 1969), p. 103.

[4] Alan K. Campbell, "Most Dynamic Sector," *National Civic Review*, 53 (February, 1964), pp. 74–75. Even taking into account that the rate of federal growth was affected by the 1952 expenditures in Korea, the rate of growth of the state and local governments far exceeded that of the national government.

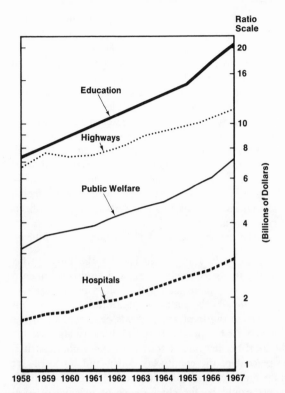

FIGURE 5–2. State General Expenditures for Selected Functions: 1958–1967. (*Source: State Government Finances in 1967*, p. 3, U.S. Department of Commerce, Bureau of the Census.)

Until the last three or four decades the states and their local governing units generally relied on separate sources of revenue. In recent years, however, there has been an increasing tendency toward the sharing of revenues through grants or subventions of funds by states to local governments. Although the pattern varies among the several states, it has become the accepted practice for the states to collect certain taxes—such as those on income, sales, and gasoline—and to share the revenue with local governments. In a number of states the principle has also been established that, because of the uneven distribution of wealth and income, funds would be allocated to the poorer communities to help them provide services comparable to those of wealthier areas.

Not only do the states share their revenue with local governments, but the federal government also makes grants to both the states and their local governing units. As Table 5–2 indicates, federal grants are not made strictly according to population, but the poorer and thinly populated states receive more on a per capita basis than the more wealthy and thickly populated states. As Figure 5–3 shows, federal grants provide more money for the states than any single state tax. Federal grants have increased sharply during the 1960s and by 1970 had reached $25 billion annually which represented 18 percent of state revenues. (See Figure 5–4.) In the past federal grants have been made for specific purposes and with restrictions regarding how the funds should be spent. State and local officials have urged that the federal government make block grants without guidelines specifying how the money may be spent. Some officials have also urged the federal government to share certain taxes it collects with state and local governments.

A brief description of the major types of state and local taxes follows.

The Property Tax. In the early years of our country the property tax provided virtually all of the funds required by state and local governments. Even at the turn of this century more than half of all state tax revenues came from this source. Gradually the states adopted other taxes and left the use of the property tax to the local governments, where it is still the major source of tax income. At the present time the property tax accounts for virtually all of the local tax revenue of townships and school districts, for approximately 90 percent of the county tax dollar, and for nearly 75 percent of municipal tax revenues. Thus, if federal and state grants were excluded, the property tax would be the chief source of revenue of local governments.

From the standpoint of taxation, property is considered to be of two types—real and personal. Real property consists of land, buildings, and other permanent fixtures. Personal property is defined as tangible—including furniture, automobiles, works of art, and jewelry—and intangible, principally stocks and bonds. Depending on state laws and local ordinances, intangible property may or may not be taxed.

A century ago property was a fairly good indicator of a person's wealth, and the property tax was not difficult to administer. Income was usually closely associated with the ownership of property, and the tax assessor could relatively easily estimate the value of real property. Unfortunately neither is the case today. The property tax is now commonly considered a regressive tax in that it places a disproportionate burden on household units, and especially on middle- and lower-income homeowners, who pay a larger proportion of their income through this tax than do more affluent indi-

TABLE 5–2. *State Allocations of Federal Aid*

States	1967 Total grants	1967 Est. population	1967 Per capita grants
Alabama	$ 491,629,000	3,558,000	$138
Alaska	118,559,000	274,000	433
Arizona	274,039,000	1,663,000	165
Arkansas	367,914,000	1,986,000	185
California	2,525,554,000	19,300,000	131
Colorado	332,677,000	2,043,000	163
Connecticut	291,170,000	2,963,000	98
Delaware	62,152,000	534,000	116
D. of C.	308,580,000	809,000	381
Florida	521,730,000	6,151,000	85
Georgia	569,017,000	4,568,000	125
Hawaii	121,977,000	780,000	156
Idaho	128,179,000	703,000	182
Illinois	1,036,270,000	10,991,000	94
Indiana	427,928,000	5,061,000	85
Iowa	393,514,000	2,774,000	142
Kansas	410,463,000	2,293,000	179
Kentucky	488,166,000	3,220,000	152
Louisiana	508,515,000	3,726,000	136
Maine	100,981,000	976,000	103
Maryland	349,795,000	3,754,000	93
Massachusetts	680,149,000	5,469,000	124
Michigan	753,947,000	8,739,000	86
Minnesota	518,861,000	3,647,000	142
Mississippi	449,964,000	2,344,000	192
Missouri	585,307,000	4,625,000	127
Montana	184,358,000	693,000	266
Nebraska	266,858,000	1,439,000	185
Nevada	76,449,000	449,000	170
New Hampshire	74,743,000	702,000	106
New Jersey	504,533,000	7,093,000	71
New Mexico	229,220,000	1,006,000	228
New York	2,162,919,000	18,078,000	120
North Carolina	522,947,000	5,122,000	102
North Dakota	224,013,000	627,000	357
Ohio	890,980,000	10,588,000	84

TABLE 5–2 (Continued)

States	1967 Total grants	1967 Est. population	1967 Per capita grants
Oklahoma	477,087,000	2,520,000	189
Oregon	289,080,000	2,008,000	144
Pennsylvania	1,081,513,000	11,728,000	92
Rhode Island	124,538,000	914,000	136
South Carolina	277,573,000	2,664,000	104
South Dakota	174,201,000	656,000	266
Tennessee	503,665,000	3,975,000	127
Texas	1,480,905,000	10,977,000	135
Utah	170,994,000	1,034,000	165
Vermont	84,460,000	425,000	199
Virginia	393,569,000	4,595,000	86
Washington	421,939,000	2,276,000	129
West Virginia	255,260,000	1,802,000	142
Wisconsin	407,689,000	4,221,000	97
Wyoming	100,111,000	315,000	318
Territories	383,233,000		
Undistributed	527,070,000		
Total	$25,106,947,000	199,861,000	$126

SOURCE: *Congressional Quarterly Weekly Report* (August 15, 1969), p. 1500, Washington, D.C.: Congressional Quarterly, Inc.

viduals. For instance, a wealthy person with resources consisting of stocks and bonds and living in an apartment pays little toward the costs of local government. As property taxes are the primary source of revenue for most local governments, the constantly rising cost of local government has fallen principally on the property owner.

In addition to being criticized as regressive, the property tax has been condemned because of the problems encountered in its administration. Appraising property is difficult because of the various types of property and the numerous factors influencing its value. Yet most tax assessors have been elected officials, and their ability to win votes has not necessarily meant that they had the technical or personal qualifications needed for an adequate performance of their responsibilities. Moreover, the ease of concealing intangible property or tangible property such as watches and jewelry usually results in real property bearing more than its share of the tax burden. Another defect of this tax is the large amount of property that

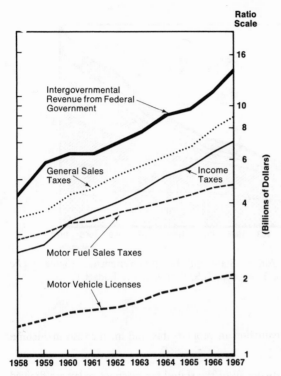

FIGURE 5–3. State General Revenue from Selected Major Sources: 1958–1967. (*Source: State Government Finances in 1967*, p. 2, U.S. Department of Commerce, Bureau of the Census.)

is exempt from taxation. In most states and communities, churches, schools, and charitable organizations are exempt from property tax, and such organizations have in some instances been able to obtain exemptions for apartment and office buildings, retirement homes, and other income-producing property that they own. Some states have also allowed property-tax exemptions to war veterans or their widows. The various exemptions, which in some cities apply to as much as one-fifth of the real property, result in a tax on other property higher than it would otherwise be. Because of the inequities of the property tax and the undue burden it places on the owners of real property, other sources of income for local governments are needed.

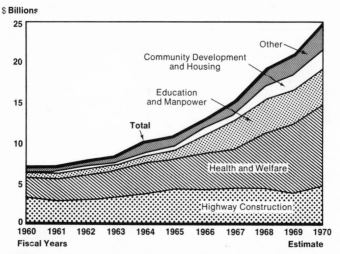

FIGURE 5–4. Federal Aid to State and Local Governments. (*Source: The Budget in Brief, Fiscal Year 1970,* U.S. Bureau of the Budget.)

Proposals include a reduction in property tax and an increase in income and sales taxes.

Income Taxes. Virtually all of the states' tax revenues today are derived from sources that they were not utilizing in 1900. The first state to adopt a permanent income tax law was Wisconsin in 1911. Since that time other states have adopted income taxes, until in 1969, thirty-nine states had imposed personal income taxes and forty-one had corporation income taxes. In addition, in some states the major cities levy a payroll tax on those who work within their environs. Today only the sales tax provides the states collectively with more tax revenue than the personal and corporation income taxes. (See Figure 5–3.)

One of the common misconceptions regarding income taxes is that the rates are always progressive; actually, a number of the states do not increase the tax rates on the higher incomes. For instance, three states tax all net personal income over $1,000 at the same rate; in those states a person pays the same tax rate whether his taxable income is the minimum $1,000 or a hundred times that. In approximately half of the other states with income taxes, the highest rate is reached at the $10,000 net income level or lower. In other states, however, the tax rate is increased on higher incomes. Largely due to the differing tax rates the proportion of a state's revenue yielded by income taxes varies considerably among the states. Whereas some states collect no income taxes, New York, Oregon, and Wisconsin each receive a major portion of their total tax revenue from this source. In recent years a number of states have adopted the practice of the federal government and have withheld personal income taxes from pay checks, thereby assuring a more even flow of revenue and preventing the avoidance of tax payments by individuals who move or live outside of the state.

The General Sales Tax. The general sales tax was used very little prior to the Depression of the 1930s, but it now produces far more state revenues than any other single tax. By 1969 all but six states—Alaska, Delaware, Montana, New Hampshire, Oregon, and Vermont—had a sales tax, and for some it provides more than half of their tax revenue. The general sales tax has the advantage of being easy and inexpensive to administer, and it furnishes huge sums of money. Because the tax paid at any one time is usually small, legislators have found that people object to it less than to the income tax. Although most states have initially established their sales taxes at 1 or 2 percent of retail sales receipts, the rates have been gradually increased, and they are now as high as 6 percent in some states.

If applied to all retail sales, the tax places the heaviest relative tax burden on those least able to pay, for low-income groups usually spend a higher proportion of their earnings than more affluent groups. To lessen the regressiveness of the tax, a number of states exempt the purchase of food and medicine. States with a sales tax generally have adopted a "use" tax, which is applied to purchases made outside the state by residents attempting to avoid the state sales tax.

Selective Sales Taxes. In addition to the general sales tax, states have imposed a "selective" sales tax, or excise tax, on numerous items, including gasoline, liquor, and tobacco. The taxes on gasoline, now the third most productive of the states' taxes, are usually earmarked along with motor-registration taxes for highways and streets on the theory that those who use the roads should pay for their construction and maintenance. Higher taxes on liquor and tobacco are often urged on the grounds that they are luxuries and that those who can afford them can also afford the tax, and that their excessive use is harmful and therefore a higher tax will reduce their use.

Other Revenue Sources. During recent years, as the people have demanded more and improved services from their state and local governments, additional funds have been required. Almost every year the state legislatures and local taxing authorities have been confronted with the task of either finding new sources of revenue or obtaining a larger yield from existing sources. Cities have installed parking meters and lots, increased their charges on municipally owned utilities, imposed new taxes on businesses and professions, instituted charges for refuse and sewage collections, and have initiated other fees and charges. States customarily tax banks and insurance companies, charge for corporation and public-utility franchises. All states except Nevada have either an inheritance or a gift tax, and many have both. States with natural resources—such as petroleum, coal, or timber—often levy a severance tax on the removal and sale of these resources; oil-rich Texas and Louisiana raise a large portion of their state income from severance taxes. Nearly one-third of the states own and operate liquor stores, and the profit as well as the tax is a source of state income; some states collect tolls for the use of certain roads and bridges; and a few have experimented with state lotteries.

chapter 6
METROPOLITAN GOVERNMENT AND PROBLEMS

American political institutions were originally designed for an agrarian society. At the time the Constitution was drafted, fewer than one American out of twenty lived in a town or city, and only two cities—New York and Philadelphia—had more than 30,000 inhabitants. During the first half of the nineteenth century, urban communities grew slowly, and most of the nation's problems were related to settling the continent and providing the limited government required by a rural economy. Andrew Jackson no doubt reflected the opinion of most of his fellow countrymen when in 1829 he told Congress: "The agricultural interest of our country is so essentially connected with every other and so superior in importance to them all that it is scarcely necessary to invite it to your particular attention."

In the decades after the Civil War the urban population grew rapidly, and America was quickly transformed from a federation of agrarian states into an industrialized and urbanized nation. When Abraham Lincoln was inaugurated in 1861, only one out of five Americans lived in urban areas, but by 1900 the proportion had changed to two out of five. Twenty years later the census report revealed for the first time that a majority of the population lived in urban communities. During recent decades the curve of urban population growth has turned sharply upward. In 1940, 56.5 percent were urban dwellers; in 1960 the percentage had increased to 69.9; and by 1970 three out of four of the nation's inhabitants were living in urban areas, comprising approximately 1.2 percent of the land. This rapid transformation of America from 95 percent rural to nearly 75 percent urban accounts for much of the growth of government and for many of the nation's problems. Yet the end has not yet been reached. In 1965 President Johnson informed Congress:

> In the remainder of this century—in less than 40 years—urban population will double, city land will double, and we will have to build in our cities as much as all that we have built since the first colonist arrived on these shores. It is as if we had 40 years to rebuild the entire urban United States.

THE NEW METROPOLIS

Urban and Metropolitan Areas

The United States Census Bureau makes a distinction between urban and metropolitan areas which must be understood in order to interpret statistics issued by the Bureau. An urban area is a community of 2,500 or more inhabitants. The Bureau has defined "standard metropolitan statistical areas" as single counties, or groups of contiguous counties,[1] which include at least one city of 50,000 persons or more, or "twin cities" with a combined population of at least 50,000. (See Figure 6–1.) The Bureau adds that for such a region to be considered a metropolitan area it must be "an integrated economic and social unit with a recognized large population nucleus." From these definitions it is apparent that there are numerous towns or small cities that are classified as urban areas but that are not part of a metropolitan area, and that within many metropolitan areas there are farms as well as towns and villages too small to be classified as urban. For instance, in 1962 half of the municipalities within metropolitan areas had less than 2,500 people each, and a fourth of the population of metropolitan areas lived outside municipalities.

In recent years much of the population growth has been in metropolitan areas. Between 1950 and 1960 metropolitan areas accounted for 84 percent of the nation's population growth. In 1950 there were 168 such areas and by 1968 there were 233 metropolitan areas in which approximately 125 million people resided. By 1980 the United States is expected to have a population of 240 million, of which three-fourths, or more than 180 million people, will reside in metropolitan areas. Ten such areas now have a population of at least 2 million persons each, and thirteen others have a population of over 1 million each. All metropolitan regions do not con-

[1] In New England, cities and towns are the components of metropolitan areas rather than counties.

sist of a large, densely populated city surrounded by suburbs. Approximately a tenth of the metropolitan areas have fewer than 100,000 inhabitants each. All states except Alaska, Vermont, and Wyoming contain at least one metropolitan area.

There is historical continuity in the urbanization of America, but there are also elements of change. The most dramatic of these are the physical differences between the city of the nineteenth century and the metropolitan area of the twentieth. Although some suburbs existed prior to World War I, the typical American city was still relatively compact. Residential neighborhoods clustered along the trolley or subway lines that radiated from the central business and industrial district. The city was coherent, directed toward and by its center, and its boundaries were clearly defined. "City limits" was the traditional last stop on the line, and a few yards away open country began.

By contrast, the modern metropolis is formless; it is a city without limits. It respects neither municipal nor county nor even state boundaries. Its growth is at the periphery rather than at the center, and its lifelines are no longer the trolley or the subway but the limited access highway. If the main characteristics of the older city were compactness and congestion, the main characteristics of the modern metropolis are diffusion and sprawl.

The Shape of the Metropolis

Metropolitan areas vary greatly. They do, however, have several common characteristics, the most obvious of which is their physical sprawl, sometimes, as in New York and Los Angeles, extending over thousands of square miles. This spreading of the urban mass has taken several forms. Around the smaller metropolitan areas, there has been a more or less "natural" growth outward from the original limits of the central city. In other areas, growth has filled in the previously undeveloped space between older commuter suburbs. In still others, a formless, highway-based leapfrogging over the existing rim of suburban settlement has left new ribbons of undeveloped space to be filled in during the next wave of expansion.

These ripples of urban growth have begun to overlap, and there are now discernible a number of nearly continuous belts of urban settlement, some of which stretch for hundreds of miles and include parts of several states. Cities blur into unincorporated but densely settled urban areas or into other cities, often with no more than a highway marker to indicate where one ends and the other begins. One such urban region, "strip city," or "megalopolis," as these urban belts have been called, stretches more than 600 miles from north of Boston to south of Richmond, Virginia, and contains more than 20 percent of the nation's population. In this mega-

FIGURE 6–1. Standard Metropolitan Statistical Areas, January, 1968. (*Source: Metropolitan Area Definition: A Re-evaluation of Concept and Statistical Practice* (Rev.), 1969, p. 22, U.S. Department of Commerce, Bureau of the Census.)

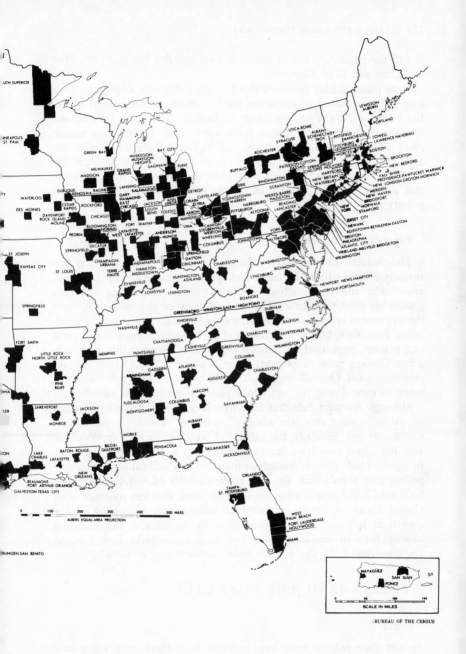

lopolis the population is as dense as in such crowded European countries as Britain and West Germany.

Some planners have predicted that by 1975 a strip city some 1,500 miles long will have snaked its way across the face of the nation from Washington north to New York, then west to Buffalo, Cleveland, Detroit, and Chicago, then down the Illinois River valley to St. Louis. Other similar clusters of population, or strip cities, will be found along the West Coast and the Gulf of Mexico. It has also been estimated that by 1975 the 14 major urban belts will hold more than 60 percent of the population and will account for more than 75 percent of the nation's economic activity.

Population Movements

The character of present-day urbanization in the United States is particularly evident within the larger metropolitan areas. The populations of many older cities have actually declined, while the outlying suburban growth has offset these losses. For example, between 1950 and 1960, 70 of the 257 central cities located within metropolitan areas declined in population. New York, Chicago, Detroit, and St. Louis were down 2, 4, 10, and 12.5 percent, respectively. Suburban populations, however, boomed: suburban Chicago grew 71 percent, for example, and the Detroit suburbs grew 79 percent. Over-all, more than two-thirds of the total national population increase during the 1950s took place in metropolitan suburbs.

Although American suburban areas have been growing more rapidly than central cities since 1900, the absolute decline of central-city populations is relatively new. Similarly, the balance of population within metropolitan areas has tipped away from the central cities only within the past few years. In 1910 central cities accounted for more than 75 percent of total metropolitan area populations. By 1965 more residents of metropolitan areas lived outside the central cities than within them. Between 1960 and 1968 United States population increased 20 million with 14 million of the growth in suburban areas. It was primarily to describe this changing balance between declining cities and booming suburbs that *Fortune* magazine coined the now-familiar term the "exploding metropolis."

PROBLEMS OF THE CORE CITY

Blight

As vast metropolitan areas have radiated from them, core cities have generally been left to face growing problems with shrinking human and material resources. Among these problems, sheer physical decay is one of the most pressing and obvious. In sections of some cities, extensive public and private urban renewal efforts have partially arrested the decline. Midtown New York, for example, is being transformed by hundreds of millions of dollars worth of new construction. In a number of other cities, striking efforts have been made or planned to rehabilitate blighted areas and to reclaim historic or distinguished buildings, as Philadelphia is doing. Compared with these scattered and partial successes, however, there are many cities that have yet to take their first serious steps against urban blight. Part of the difficulty is the high cost of even first steps. A recent study estimates that $42 billion a year above current construction expenditures would be needed to bring American cities up to a "modest standard" of adequacy within the next decade. With the flight of wealth and people to the suburbs continuing, the achievement of even a "modest standard" is plainly far beyond any purely local resources that might conceivably be made available for the task.

The federal government, which has assisted in slum clearance and urban renewal projects since the early 1950s, has initiated the "model city," or "demonstration city," program. Under this program, which was authorized by the Demonstration Cities and Metropolitan Development Act of 1966, cities may compete for federal funds by submitting plans for renewal and redevelopment. Due largely to increased expenditures for national security, Congress has appropriated much less for such projects than most students of metropolitan government believe desirable, but by 1969 planning grants had been awarded to 150 communities.

Economic Anemia

Spreading urban blight has been both cause and consequence of the economic decline that many older cities have suffered, particularly in their central business districts. In these densely built-up areas, most of the important indexes of economic vitality—factory production, commercial construction, retail sales, bank deposits, and a number of others—have shown absolute or relative decreases in recent years. In one five-year period in the thirty largest metropolitan areas, the central city areas lost approximately 50,000 wholesale trade jobs. Moreover, this creeping anemia feeds upon itself. Business and people leave downtown; their departure generates further decay, which prompts others to follow those who have already left. Unchecked decay of the traditional urban core not only disfigures the city but also erodes the tax base from which the city must support its resurgence.

Although shrinking tax bases are of most immediate concern to the cities, they also affect other levels of government as well. Cities have traditionally paid far more in direct state and county taxes than they have received in benefits. State aid for schools and highways, for example, is disproportionately financed from taxes collected in cities, and spent in rural and suburban areas. In addition, cities provide a variety of indirect subsidies to suburban areas. In some states, cities are obliged to furnish water, power, sewage disposal, and other services to noncity areas at or below cost. Cities are also practically obliged to maintain public transportation, health, safety, and other services to meet the needs of commuter populations.

Dependency and Ethnicity

Despite depopulation, shrinking tax bases, and physical decay, American cities are being called upon to render more and better services to populations increasingly dependent on them. Baltimore, for example, lost 3 percent of its population between 1950 and 1960, yet city spending for education, welfare, police and fire protection, health, and hospitals more than doubled during the decade. The case is not unique among aging core cities.

The seeming paradox of costlier government for fewer people results from rising service standards and from the changing social composition of the older central cities. These cities are increasingly becoming places for those who are too poor to leave them, who are unwelcome elsewhere, or who can afford the costly amenities that will insulate them to some degree from the more objectionable features of city life. Mayor John V. Lindsay has commented that almost 2 million New Yorkers were "locked in poverty" and that their plight was the most serious problem facing his city. Another difficult problem is the disproportionate increase in urban nonwhite populations. For instance, in a ten-year period New York City's white population diminished by nearly a million and in the same time the city's Negro and Puerto Rican population increased by virtually the same amount. More than half of the population of Washington, D.C., is now black and, according to projections of the U.S. Census Bureau, if the present trends continue, by 1984 Negroes will constitute a majority of the inhabitants of several other cities including Baltimore, Chicago, Cleveland, Detroit, Jacksonville, Oakland, Philadelphia, New Orleans, and St. Louis. Unemployment rates are approximately twice as high for urban Negroes as for urban whites, a reflection of both educational deficiencies and job discrimination.

One point, however, should be made clear. The classic dichotomy of the central city as the home of the underprivileged, the poor, and the nonwhite, and the suburbs as the home of the middle- or upper-class white does not apply to all metropolitan areas, but it does apply to most large areas of half a million inhabitants or more and to many other metropolitan areas in the Northeast. In the medium and small metropolitan areas outside the Northeast, individuals with high and low socioeconomic status are found both in the central city and in the suburbs. In the West and South low-income nonwhites are more typically found in suburbs than in the core city.

Leadership in the Changing City

Racial tension and financial deficits in municipal budgets are not the only consequences of the great city's changing class and ethnic structure. The spontaneous generation of leadership from within the complex substructure of society has long been one of the hallmarks of American democracy. What happens when the middle- and upper-class groups, which have traditionally assumed this leadership, leave the cities for the suburbs and are replaced in part by citizens who may be neither able nor inclined to assume it? On one level, nothing may happen, at least immediately. In the face of physical decay, social upheaval, and staggering financial problems, many of our major cities are now governed as well as at any time in their histories. In city after city the electorate has chosen mayors as competent as any who have ever occupied the office.

City government, of course, is more than a dynamic mayor; it is also the extensive administrative establishment that is needed to render the many services that citizens expect their city to provide, and here, too, the city is better served than ever before. The traditional boss-dominated big city political machine, based on patronage, favoritism, and corruption, was professional in its politics but, by modern standards, rankly amateur in its administration. By contrast, city government today works primarily through professional bureaucracies recruited on the basis of merit and protected from political interference and dismissal. Where the big city machine of another era dispensed favors to needy or deserving partisans, the administrative city dispenses needed services on a nonpartisan basis to qualified citizens. If politics in the conventional sense has not vanished from the city, it is plainly blander and less pervasive than it was.

But there are clouds on the horizon. While city government is more professional (and considerably more costly) than it was under machine control, it also engages less of our loyalty and time. This applies not only to the formal institutions of government, in which we participate by voting, and perhaps officeholding, but also to the elaborate web of private associations which flow from and support these formal institutions. In many cities nominations for elective office or for membership on citizen boards and commissions are no longer widely sought. Party organizations and non-partisan civic groups in cities across the country report increasing difficulty in recruiting workers. To a disturbing extent, the traditional springs of civic leadership give evidence of running dry. The potential civic leaders who leave the city altogether, or who still work in the city but live and pay taxes elsewhere, are no longer deeply absorbed in the city's problems and affairs, and the newer urban migrants, more dependent on the city than absorbed in it, have not yet filled the void.

SUBURBIA: IMPERFECT PARADISE

Why the Growth of Suburbs

Like the larger metropolitan areas of which they are a part, suburbs are of many types and sizes. The suburb itself is not wholly a twentieth-century phenomenon. In the last quarter of the nineteenth century the development of commuter railroad lines or main-line commuter services enabled the first residential suburbs to form and grow beyond the city's limits. The principal motive underlying the settlement of these early suburban communities was not so much to extend the city as to escape it, and only those could escape who could pay their way. Thus the residential suburbs that first sprang up around New York, Boston, Philadelphia, and Chicago were generally designed by and for those well-to-do or solid middle-class city-dwellers who were able and willing to endure a daily train ride for the comparative ease and privacy of suburban living.

Although the basic motive of escaping from the congestion, rush, and squalor of the city is still very much at work, the spectacular growth of suburban areas in recent years also reflects the improved economic condition of millions of Americans. Since 1945 many Americans have left the cities for the suburbs, hoping to find there open space, pure air, safe streets, and good schools that the city seemed unable to offer.

The Role of the Automobile

Underlying the dramatic growth of the dispersed metropolis is the larger number of Americans owning automobiles. Our population is approximately 50 percent larger than it was only twenty years ago, but there are nearly three times as many cars. The automobile allows millions of Americans to live truly metropolitan lives—living and sending their children to school in one governmental jurisdiction, earning their livings in another, shopping in a third, and seeking recreation in a fourth. As the earlier suburbs were primarily railroad-based, the metropolitan suburbs of today are possible because of the automobile. The automobile-age suburb has both caused and followed extension of the road grid: the farther the grid is extended the greater the demands put upon it for further extension. While this process has supported suburban growth, it has created serious problems for cities like New York, where every new bridge, tunnel, or express access route seems only to increase midtown congestion, and where horse-drawn traffic moved almost twice as quickly sixty years ago as automobile traffic moves now.

Economic Trends and Suburbs

Basic economic trends have also contributed to the "exploding metropolis." Changing industrial technology and plant requirements, along with a general tendency toward decentralization, have nourished the movement of many established industries from aging multistoried downtown factories to new one-story plants in suburban "industrial parks." The increasing reliance on truck rather than rail transportation has worked to the same end. In the newer space-age industries with high proportions of well-educated and well-paid workers, attractive suburban locations are preferred not only for their convenience but also as a means of bidding against competing employers for personnel. Retail and financial establishments, service trades, and other forms of business activity have also followed the movement of population to the suburbs. Suburban land is cheaper and more plentiful; taxes are lower, at least initially; suburban locations offer easier access and parking to buyers, users, and clientele, and more pleasant working environments for employees.

There has also been an element of physical necessity in the continuing suburban boom. The number of family units in the nation has sharply increased, and the fact that many of the older central cities are almost completely built up has spurred the development of outlying areas where land was still available.

The Penalties of Growth

The suburbs are the growing edge of America, and the costs of growth are high. Ideally, physical development should go hand in hand with the formation of local governments competent to anticipate, understand, and direct it. Unfortunately, the ideal is not often realized. In the more extreme cases, hit-and-run development has left the land scarred with isolated clusters of cramped and graceless tract houses, dumped haphazardly wherever the price of land was low and land use controls were negligible. Often these previously undeveloped areas do not have the kind of schools, utilities, or police and fire protection that most Americans would regard as adequate. Such areas are, in a very real sense, blighted from the beginning, and the eventual formation of a nominal town or city government may not by itself create a viable community.

The newer suburbs have bloomed on the hope that services would be better, costs lower, and life in general more satisfying than in the city. Bringing such miracles to pass is quite another matter. The alternatives often are to trim services to available funds, to maintain standards and raise taxes accordingly, or to rely on volunteer effort and hope for the best. Amateurism in the conduct of public business is not what most communities want, but it is frequently all that they are willing or able to support.

The Politics of Suburbia

The politics of suburbia are varied, but there are certain common characteristics. One of the most prominent of these is an element of artificiality in much of our suburban government and politics. Historically, local governments in the United States have developed naturally to meet the common needs of distinct and cohesive communities. Changing values and modern transportation have now broken down the older limits of community. When we no longer work where we live, we are not fully citizens of either place; and when this separation is reinforced by a bewildering hodgepodge of arbitrarily defined governmental jurisdictions, the idea that local government should be rooted in local needs may lose much of its appeal. With incorporation procedures as they are in most states, suburban cities can be formed whenever enough people occupy the requisite space. But people living in physical proximity do not by themselves make complete communities, although they are obviously the nucleus around which such communities may eventually form. For much of suburban America, however, this evolution has not yet taken place, and for much of it, it never will. In this respect, the city and the suburb may be quite different. The New Yorker is a New Yorker all of the time. Westport, Levittown, and Oak Park cannot yet demand of their citizens an equal attachment.

The politics of suburbia in many ways reflect this lack of community commitment. Although there are differences from place to place, there is a marked national preference for nonpartisanship in suburban politics, and for professional management in suburban government. For many suburbs, "nonpartisanship" does not mean an absence of political activity, but only that state and national parties and party positions do not often figure prominently in their public decisions. In such areas, people influential in the community replace political leaders.

The emphasis upon professional management, best expressed in the growing suburban attachment to the manager plan of government, goes hand and glove with formal nonpartisanship. For many suburbanites, the manager system represents "good government" without the presumed taint of "politics." But government *is* politics, and an absence of overt political activity or leadership does not alter the fact. Although many suburban communities have adopted the plan prematurely, a manager can give a community efficient administration. He should not be expected to do more. At best, he is an adjunct to, and not a subsitute for, a healthy political process.

METROPOLITAN GOVERNMENT: THE PATTERN OF DISPERSION

In economic and human terms, the metropolis is a web of interdependent relationships. In governmental terms, the metropolis is a chaos of competing and limited jurisdictions, few, if any, of which extend throughout the entire metropolitan area. The metropolitan area is a socioeconomic reality, but it has no political identity, consciousness, or form. As one student of metropolitan government has written: "The metropolitan area has no capital, courthouse, or city hall, no corporate existence, no body, no soul, no sense of being, indeed no being in any concrete meaning of the term."[2] In brief, this gap between one metropolitan community and many metropolitan governments is the real core of the metropolitan problem.

Residents of metropolitan areas are taxed, if not governed, by a bewildering number of governments—town, city, township, special district, and county. Although individual metropolitan areas differ widely in the complexity of their governmental arrangements, the trend has been increasingly toward the proliferation of units. In 1960 within the 212 metropolitan areas there were 18,442 independent government units. Eleven metropolitan areas each contained more than 250 units of local government; and each of another 13 areas could claim from 200 to 249 units. In general, the larger the metropolitan area, the more governments will be found within it. The Chicago metropolitan area surpassed all others with 1,060 local governments, but Philadelphia with 963 was not far behind.[3]

Why So Many Governments?

The large number of local governments results from the sheer scale and

[2] Roscoe C. Martin, *Metropolis in Transition: Local Government Adaptation to Changing Urban Needs*, Washington, D.C.: Government Printing Office, 1963, p. 141.

[3] U.S. Bureau of the Census, *Census of Governments*, 1962, Vol. V, p. 3.

diversity of the modern metropolis. The component parts of any metropolitan area belong to the same regional community and have many common interests and problems, but it is their differences—often slight or fancied—which underlie much of the "balkanization" of government that marks the metropolis.

The traditional distrust of most Americans for "large" or "distant" units of government has also encouraged governmental separatism. A preference for local autonomy and self-government is deeply rooted in the American tradition. Although constitutional and statutory requirements vary considerably from state to state, they are generally quite permissive with respect to the creation of new units of government. Given the choice between forming their own local governments or casting their lot with established jurisdictions such as the city or the county, the residents of developing metropolitan communities have typically chosen to form a new unit of government.

Disadvantages of Governmental Fragmentation

The penalties of metropolitan dispersion include the excessive cost of urban services performed by units too small to render them economically or well. Although there is an emotional appeal to "local government," there is generally a point at which the economies of scale overweigh the appeal and advantages of local autonomy and control. Adequate police and fire protection, for example, require capital investment for buildings, vehicles, and communications equipment far beyond the reach of the typical suburban community.

In the end, governmental fragmentation in metropolitan areas may frustrate some of the very purposes that give rise to it. One of the principal values underlying the recent growth of suburbia has been the hope of re-creating there the kind of town meeting democracy that we like to think dealt openly and well with the problems of an earlier time. But the modern American metropolis is not colonial New England, and nostalgia or myopia will not make it so. As metropolitan governments multiply and assume more complex and technical responsibilities, citizen interest and involvement typically diminish in roughly inverse ratio. Taxes, schools, race relations, and other issues from time to time generate some excitement, but political indifference and withdrawal are increasingly evident in every metropolis. For instance, in city and suburban general elections turnout is often less than 25 percent of the voters.

SOLUTIONS TO METROPOLITAN PROBLEMS

Reorganization of Metropolitan Government

Obviously many problems of the metropolis cannot be satisfactorily solved by the myriad units of local governments as they are now organized. Many approaches for reorganizing governments in metropolitan areas to strengthen their capacity for handling metropolitan problems have been tried or suggested. In general, these proposals involve transferring functions from one local government to another, creating new governmental units, coordinating local governments, or making joint agreements. A brief survey is presented here of the principal approaches that are available.

Annexation. Annexing the adjacent territory has been the traditional method for adjusting the boundaries of municipalities to urban growth. Most major cities have reached their present size by this means. During the nineteenth century and the early 1900s annexations were more common than in more recent years. However, various cities in the past two decades have enlarged their boundaries by this method. For instance, in 1960 Kansas City, Missouri, more than doubled its size by annexing 187 square miles of territory. Annexation is usually feasible only if the suburban areas are unincorporated, for most cities prefer to maintain their separate status to being absorbed by the central city. Because many major cities are virtually surrounded today by municipalities, annexation does not provide a practical means for securing the political unification of most metropolitan districts.

City-County Consolidation. City-county consolidation or separating the city from the county have long been advocated as means of integrating local government functions. Prior to 1900 four cities—Baltimore, Denver, St. Louis, and San Francisco—were split from the remainder of their counties and established as separate governments. Except in Virginia, which permits all cities of 10,000 or more population to separate from the counties, there were few attempts to effect city-county separations or consolidations during this century. However, in 1949 Baton Rouge, Louisiana, merged with its county, in 1962 Nashville and Davidson County, Tennessee, consolidated, and in 1966 Jacksonville and Duval

County, Florida, merged. Several other efforts at city-county consolidation have been defeated recently by the local electorates.[4]

If a city or metropolitan area comprises the greater part of a county or can readily be separated from the county, the formation of a city-county government may offer certain advantages. It has particular appeal to the citizens who object to paying taxes for the salaries of two sets of officials performing similar or duplicating tasks, such as a chief of police and a sheriff, a city attorney and a county district attorney, and a city and a county superintendent of schools. Some disadvantages may result from city-county consolidation. For example, if the metropolitan areas spill over into adjacent counties, as is the case in the San Francisco Bay region and other areas, city-county consolidation may hinder future efforts at metropolitan integration. Also, splitting a city from the county may seriously reduce the remaining tax resources of the county.

Special Districts. Numerous limited-pupose districts have been established usually to perform some service such as fire protection, transportation, sanitation, or recreation. The great majority serve only a small area, but some function throughout a large region. Examples of large, single-purpose metropolitan districts are the Massachusetts Bay Transit Authority, the Metropolitan Water District of Southern California, the Cleveland Metropolitan Park District, and the Port of New York Authority. There are several advantages to this governmental device. It is easily created, usually by an act of the state legislature, and it may unify the administration of a large-scale activity of concern to individuals living in areas encompassing several local governments. There are, however, disadvantages to special districts as they have been organized. The large number of them complicate the problem of governmental coordination and make it more difficult for the citizenry to understand and exercise effective control over local government.

The multipurpose district has been proposed as one of the most promising approaches for metropolitan regions, especially for those areas covering more than one county. It has the advantage of the single-purpose district without creating a further fractionalization of government in the metropolitan area. To date the only example of a multipurpose district is the municipality of Metropolitan Seattle. This district was established in 1958 by a state law that permits the cities and towns in the Seattle metropolitan area to join together to provide essential services including mass transportation, parks, water supply, and garbage disposal.

[4] The following attempts at city-county consolidation were defeated by the local electorates: Albuquerque-Bernalillo County, New Mexico (1959); Knoxville-Knox County, Tennessee (1959); Macon-Bibb County, Georgia (1960); Durham-Durham County, North Carolina (1961); and Richmond-Henrico County, Virginia (1961).

Federation. Similar to the multipurpose district plan is the proposal to reorganize metropolitan governments according to the federated or borough system. This approach provides for the division of metropolitan governmental functions between two levels of government, somewhat comparable to the division of functions between the national government and the states. Strictly local functions and services would be left to the municipalities, and area-wide functions would be delegated to the "metropolitan" government. Those who advocate this plan assert that it has the merit of retaining the identity of the local governments and local participation in public affairs but permits the handling of services and activities of interest to the entire area by the central government. No American metropolitan area has yet adopted a metropolitan federation, although the Dade County, Florida, metropolitan government contains several features of such a system. Two Canadian cities—Toronto and Winnipeg—have established federated governments that have operated quite successfully.

Local Intergovernmental Agreements and Cooperation. Local communities in metropolitan areas have devised a number of means of cooperating. Many metropolitan councils have been formed. These are voluntary associations of elected officials, who meet to discuss common problems and seek a consensus. Typically they are composed of the chief elected officials of the local government and occasionally they include certain state officials. Some councils have representatives of local governments in two or more states. Examples of metropolitan councils are the Puget Sound Governmental Conference, Metropolitan Atlanta Council of Local Governments, Southern California Association of Governments, Metropolitan Washington (D.C.) Council of Governments, and the Metropolitan Regional Council (New York, New Jersey, and Connecticut).

A second type of cooperation is found where a local government conducts an activity jointly with one or more other governments, or contracts with another government for the performance of a public function. Often two or more cities cooperate to establish a water system, hospital, or airport. Another example of intergovernmental cooperation is the supply of services by the central cities to their suburbs; these include such services as public transportation, library facilities, or sewage disposal. For instance, a recent survey of intergovernmental contracts indicated that Cleveland had more than thirty contracts with its suburbs.

A typical approach is the gradual and piecemeal transfer of functions from cities to the county. In several metropolitan areas the counties have assumed the responsibility for such programs as public health, welfare, library services, and recreational programs. Los Angeles County, in particular, has contracted to perform a large number of services for its municipalities. Under the Lakewood Plan, named after the city which originated the idea, a city may contract with the county for virtually all of its governmental services.

The assumption of urban functions by Dade County, Florida, has been watched with much interest. Under the Dade County metropolitan charter, adopted by the local voters in 1959, the county is responsible for a substantial number of governmental activities and services including water supply, sewage disposal, air pollution control, building and zoning codes, fire and police protection, housing and urban renewal, and transportation. The municipalities retain control over local matters not delegated to the county, but the county may take over a function from the city if it does not maintain a minimum level of performance.

During recent decades, in virtually every major metropolis studies have been conducted and plans submitted for reorganizing and rationalizing the government. Most of the proposals which provided for major changes— such as city-county consolidation or the establishment of a federated government—have been rejected by the local electorates. Because of these experiences it seems reasonable to predict that in most metropolitan areas governmental reforms will not come through radical changes but through informal cooperation, piecemeal changes, and gradual adjustments.

State and National Roles

The responsibilities of the states for metropolitan areas are varied. Because the local governments receive their powers from the states, any major change in their governmental structure must have the approval of the state legislature and governor. State governments have assumed direct responsibility for certain operations, such as highway construction, which earlier were performed by localities; and other functions will probably be assumed by the states. The states have attempted to assist their metropolitan areas in other ways, including providing financial assistance, creating regional planning agencies, adopting measures for water and air pollution control, establishing special metropolitan authorities, and assisting in the planning of entire new communities.

The federal government in recent years has been increasingly involved in problems of the metropolis, and a still more expanded role by the federal government may be expected. The establishment of the Departments of Housing and Urban Development and Transportation and the establishment of the Urban Affairs Council within the Executive Office of the President are evidence of the general awareness that problems of urban areas cannot be solved by the state and local governments alone. There are now more than thirty interstate metropolitan areas comprising a population in excess of 40 million; and as the number of metropolitan areas covering parts of two or more states increases, more demands will be made for action by the federal government. For example, due to the increasing protests over air pollution in several interstate metropolitan areas, Congress has enacted legislation aimed at dealing with the problem. Moreover, many problems of intrastate metropolitan regions require federal attention. New York's Mayor Lindsay has called for "a new kind of federalism, in which the national government will have to coordinate and finance the programs necessary to make our cities livable, but in which local initiative and control will become the ultimate sources of decision."

Although the federal government will probably become more directly involved in the metropolis, its present role consists primarily of providing financial assistance for programs administered by local and state governments. In 1969 there were more than seventy federal programs that supported urban development, as well as several other types of federal aid for governments in metropolitan areas. Included among the federal programs were grants for a wide range of activities such as housing, transportation, urban planning, airports, schools, hospitals, urban renewal, space acquisition, recreation, and air- and water-pollution control. The National Committee on Urban Growth has recommended federal funding to build ten cities to accommodate at least a million persons each and a hundred cities for at least a hundred thousand persons each. In Great Britain twenty-four new cities have been built since World War II to drain off excess growth in large cities and to save the countryside from suburban sprawl.

Although state and federal programs help solve some metropolitan problems, they also further complicate certain political and governmental issues. As the Advisory Commission on Intergovernmental Relations has noted,

> In the course of supplying needed help, federal and state programs threaten to push the confused governmental situation closer to a state of chaos. Coordination of efforts is a prime requirement for effective government action in metropolitan areas; yet the problems of coordination are compounded by the addition of higher levels of government to the fragmented local scene.

State and federal programs also raise the issue of citizen control of metropolitan government. In appraising any proposal involving the metropolitan scene, consideration should be given both to the effective performance of the necessary governmental functions and to the popular control of government. Most proposals have been aimed primarily at either assisting in the financing of programs or achieving greater administrative efficiency. But in the metropolis of today the issue of stimulating citizen interest and participation in civic affairs may be more perplexing than obtaining adequate financing or efficiency and economy in government. Hence, in assessing any new program or suggested governmental reform a basic consideration should be whether it contributes to popular interest in, and control of, the political processes.

BIBLIOGRAPHY

CHAPTER 1 STATE CONSTITUTIONAL
AND POLITICAL SYSTEMS

Agger, Robert E., et al. *The Rulers and the Ruled: Political Power and Impotence in American Communities*. New York: Wiley, 1964.

Allen, Tip H., Jr., and Coleman B. Ransome, Jr. *Constitutional Revision in Theory and Practice*. University, Ala.: University of Alabama Press, 1962.

Anderson, William. *The States and the Nation, Rivals or Partners*. Minneapolis: University of Minnesota Press, 1955.

Banfield, Edward C., and James Q. Wilson. *City Politics*. Cambridge, Mass.: Harvard University Press, 1963.

Council of State Governments. *State Government: An Annotated Bibliography*. Chicago: Council of State Governments, 1959. Revised periodically.

Crews, Robert E., Jr. *State Politics, Readings on Political Behavior*. Belmont, Calif.: Wadsworth, 1968.

Dahl, Robert A. *Who Governs?* New Haven, Conn.: Yale University Press, 1961.

Dishman, Robert B. *State Constitutions: The Shape of the Document*. New York: National Municipal League, 1960.

Elazar, Daniel J. *American Federalism: A View from the States*. New York: Crowell, 1966.

Fenton, John H. *Midwest Politics*. New York: Holt, Rinehart and Winston, 1966.

Graves, W. Brooke. *American Intergovernmental Relations*. New York: Scribner's, 1964.

Graves, W. Brooke (ed.). *Major Problems in State Constitutional Revision*.

Chicago: Public Administration Service, 1960.

Hunter, Floyd. *Community Power Structure: A Study of Decision Makers.* Chapel Hill, N.C.: University of North Carolina Press, 1953.

Jacob, Herbert, and Kenneth Vines (eds.). *Politics in the American States.* Boston: Little, Brown, 1965.

Lockard, Duane. *New England State Politics.* Princeton, N.J.: Princeton University Press, 1959.

National Municipal League. *The Model State Constitution,* 6th ed. New York: National Municipal League, 1963.

CHAPTER 2   THE LEGISLATIVE PROCESS
IN THE STATES

Adrian, Charles R. *State and Local Governments,* 2d ed. New York: McGraw-Hill, 1967.

Baker, Gordon E. *State Constitutions: Reapportionment.* New York: National Municipal League, 1960.

Council of State Governments. *American Legislatures: Structures and Procedures.* Chicago: Council of State Governments, 1959.

Fordham, Jefferson B. *The State Legislative Institution.* Philadelphia: University of Pennsylvania Press, 1959.

Heard, Alexander (ed.). *State Legislatures in American Politics.* Englewood Cliffs, N.J.: Prentice-Hall, 1966.

Jewell, Malcolm E. *The State Legislature.* New York: Random House, 1962.

Key, V. O., Jr. *American State Politics: An Introduction.* New York: Knopf, 1956.

Munger, Frank (ed.). *American State Politics: Readings for Comparative Analysis.* New York: Crowell, 1966.

Sorauf, Frank J. *Party and Representation: Legislative Politics in Pennsylvania,* New York: Atherton Press, 1963.

Wahlke, John C., *et al. The Legislative System.* New York: Wiley, 1962.

Walker, Harvey. *Executive-Legislative Relations.* New York: National Municipal League, 1959.

CHAPTER 3   STATE EXECUTIVES
AND JUDGES

Abraham, Henry J. *The Judicial Process.* New York: Oxford University Press, 1962.

Brooks, Glenn E. *When Governors Convene: The Governors' Conference and National Politics.* Baltimore: Johns Hopkins Press, 1961.

Council of State Governments. *Book of the States.* Chicago: Council of State Governments. Published biennially.

Jacob, Herbert. *Justice in America.* Boston: Little, Brown, 1965.

Kallenbach, Joseph E. *The American Chief Executive*. New York: Harper & Row, 1966.

Lipson, Leslie. *The American Governor: From Figurehead to Leader*. Chicago: University of Chicago Press, 1939.

Mayer, Lewis. *The American Legal System*, rev. ed. New York: Harper & Row. 1964.

Murphy, Walter F., and C. Herman Pritchett. *Courts, Judges and Politics*. New York: Random House, 1961.

Ransome, Coleman B., Jr. *The Office of the Governor in the United States*. University, Ala.: University of Alabama Press, 1956.

Rich, Bennett M. *State Constitutions: The Governor*. New York: National Municipal League, 1960.

Sace, Homer E. *The Organization of the Executive Office of the Governor*. New York: Institute of Public Administration, 1950.

Schlesinger, Joseph A. *How They Became Governor*. East Lansing: Michigan State University Press, 1957.

CHAPTER 4 LOCAL GOVERNMENT

Bollens, John C. *Special District Governments in the United States*. Berkeley: University of California Press, 1957.

Booth, David A. (ed.). *Council-Manager Government, 1960–1964: An Annotated Bibliography*. Chicago: International City Manager's Association, 1965.

Dye, Thomas R. *Politics in States and Communities*. Englewood Cliffs, N.J.: Prentice-Hall, 1969.

Grant, Daniel R., and H. C. Nixon. *State and Local Government in America*. Boston: Allyn and Bacon, 1968.

Kneier, Charles M. *City Government in the United States*. New York: Harper & Row, 1957.

Lockard, Duane. *The Politics of State and Local Government*. New York: Macmillan, 1969.

Morlan, Robert L. *Capitol, Courthouse, and City Hall: Readings in American State and Local Government*, 2d ed. Boston: Houghton Mifflin, 1966.

Press, Charles, and Oliver P. Williams (eds.). *Democracy in the Fifty States*. Chicago: Rand McNally, 1966.

Scientific American Editors. *Cities*. New York: Knopf, 1965.

Snider, Clyde F., and Samuel K. Gore. *American State and Local Government*, 2d ed. New York: Appleton-Century-Crofts, 1965.

U.S. Department of Commerce, Bureau of the Census. *Census of Governments, 1967: Elective Officials of State and Local Governments*. Washington, D.C.: Government Printing Office, 1967.

U.S. Department of Commerce, Bureau of the Census. *Census of Governments, 1962: Governmental Organization*. Washington, D.C.: Government Printing Office, 1963.

CHAPTER 5   STATE AND LOCAL
FUNCTIONS AND SERVICES

Advisory Commission on Intergovernmental Relations. *Tax Overlapping in the United States*. Washington, D.C.: U.S. Government Printing Office, 1966.

Blair, George S. *American Local Government*. New York: Harper & Row, 1964.

Committee for Economic Development. *Modernizing State Government*. New York: Committee for Economic Development, 1967.

Conant, James Bryant. *Shaping of Educational Policy*. New York: McGraw-Hill, 1964.

Fesler, James W. (ed.). *The 50 States and Their Local Governments*. New York: Knopf, 1967.

Groves, Harold M. *Financing Government*, 6th ed. New York: Holt, Rinehart and Winston, 1964.

Hawley, Willis D. (ed.). *Where Governments Meet: Emerging Patterns of Intergovernmental Relations*. Berkeley, Calif.: Institute of Governmental Studies, 1967.

Martin, Roscoe C. *The Cities and the Federal System*. New York: Atherton Press, 1965.

Mitau, G. Theodore. *State and Local Government: Politics and Processes*. New York: Scribner's, 1966.

Mosher, Frederick C., and Orville F. Poland. *The Costs of American Governments*. New York: Dodd, Mead, 1964.

U.S. Department of Commerce, Bureau of the Census. *State Finances in 1966*. Washington, D.C.: Government Printing Office, 1967.

CHAPTER 6   METROPOLITAN GOVERNMENT
AND PROBLEMS

Abrams, Charles. *The City is the Frontier*. New York: Harper & Row, 1965.

Advisory Commission on Intergovernmental Relations. *Metropolitan America: Challenge to Federalism*. (Report submitted to the Committee on Government Operations. 89th Congress, 2d Session) Washington, D.C.: Government Printing Office, 1966.

Bollens, John C. (ed.). *Exploring the Metropolitan Community*. Berkeley, Calif.: University of California Press, 1961.

Bollens, John C., and Henry J. Schmandt. *The Metropolis*. New York: Harper & Row, 1965.

Campbell, Alan K., and Seymour Sacks. *Metropolitan America: Fiscal Patterns and Governmental Systems*. New York: Free Press, 1967.

Connery, Robert H., and Richard H. Leach. *The Federal Government and Metropolitan Areas*. Cambridge, Mass.: Harvard University Press, 1960.

Coulter, Philip B. *Politics of Metropolitan Areas*. New York: Crowell, 1967.

Danielson, Michael N. (ed.). *Metropolitan Politics*. Boston: Little, Brown, 1966.

Goldwin, Robert A. (ed.). A Nation of Cities. Chicago: Rand McNally, 1968.

Goodall, Leonard E. The American Metropolis. Columbus, Ohio: Merrill, 1968.

Gottman, Jean. Megalopolis: The Urbanized Northeastern Seaboard. New York: Twentieth Century Fund, 1961.

Greer, Scott. Governing the Metropolis. New York: Wiley, 1962.

Jacobs, Philip E., and James V. Toscano (eds.). The Integration of Political Communities. New York: Lippincott, 1964.

Martin, Roscoe C. The Cities and the Federal System. New York: Atherton, 1965.

Sayre, Wallace C., and Herbert Kaufman. Governing New York City. New York: Russell Sage Foundations, 1960.

Weaver, Robert C. Dilemmas of Urban America. Cambridge, Mass.: Harvard University Press, 1965.

Wood, Robert C. Suburbia: Its People and Their Politics. Boston: Houghton Mifflin, 1958.

INDEX